Timeless Halloween Collectibles

1920 to 1949

A Halloween Reference Book from the Beistle Company Archives with Price Guide

Claire M. Lavin

Schiffer Publishing Ltd

4880 Lower Valley Road · Atglen, PA 19310

Dedication

To my husband, Philip Andrew Lavin

I couldn't have done this without you, both literally and figuratively. Since our reintroduction, I've had the opportunity of capturing your heart and infusing it with the mysterious colors of orange and black. A passion for Halloween collecting is one thing, but introducing it into our home's year-round décor is another, and not once have you uttered a word of complaint. You are the best thing that has ever happened to me: my partner and support, my cheerleader, and always, my Love. Throughout this whole Halloween adventure, you have been my #1 fan and that means everything to me. ...And yes dear, I do love you more!

Library of Congress Control Number: 2004109760

Designed by John P. Cheek
Cover design by Bruce Waters
Type set in Kabel Bd/Korinna BT

ISBN: 978-0-7643-2146-7
Printed in China
5 4 3 2

Published by Schiffer Publishing Ltd.
4880 Lower Valley Road
Atglen, PA 19310
Phone: (610) 593-1777; Fax: (610) 593-2002
E-mail: Info@schifferbooks.com

For the largest selection of fine reference books on this and related subjects, please visit our web site at
www.schifferbooks.com
We are always looking for people to write books on new and related subjects. If you have an idea for a book please contact us at the above address.

This book may be purchased from the publisher.
Please try your bookstore first.
You may write for a free catalog.

Contents

Acknowledgments

In all honesty, I feel a bit uncomfortable in wearing the mantle called "author." In truth, the Beistle Company wrote this book. All information contained within these pages was literally taken from the company's archives of catalogues and material. Some of the written descriptions contained in the Beistle Product Catalogues were so priceless that there was no question of my not including them. I've added my comments here and there and have included an estimated value for the Halloween items to round out the information.

Of course, the information in this book would never have been made available to the public without the generosity and cooperation of the wonderful people at the Beistle Company. My thanks go out to Tricia Lacy, President; Rick Buterbaugh, Art Director; Terriann Hilbinger, Assistant Art Director; Matt Peters, Artist Assistant; Dan Kauffman, Die Shop; Tim Alleman, Assistant Supervisor; Sharon Foust, Operator; and especially Bob Hansen, Illustrator, who worked with us throughout the entire process and to whom both Phil and I are indebted for his knowledge, expertise, and tireless spirit. I think it's safe to say that I may have made Bob my newest convert into the wonderful world of vintage Halloween collecting!

This book would never have come into being if it weren't for the persistent urgings of both my sister, Kathleen ("Kate") Zimmerman, and my good friend and fellow antiques dealer, Barbara J. Wachter, that "you've got to write a book!" So, here it is you two! A special thank you to Barbara's husband, Robert Wachter, for both his time and legal expertise. What a generous person! Speaking of benevolent, a big hug and kiss for Gerard Gantert (the "Ger") for use of his photographic supplies and equipment that made my job of cataloguing all those slides a much easier one. Danke! While we're on the subject of photography and the like, a very special nod of the head to Philip A. Lavin, my husband, who undertook the assignment of photographing. He took on a yeoman's task and his work showcases just one of his many, many talents. And I would be remiss if I didn't mention Maria T. Hobson and her wealth of knowledge and skills when it came to getting this book in some sort of semblance for presentation to my Schiffer editor. To say that I'm forever indebted wouldn't begin to cover all you've done for me. Thanks Ri-z!

If space allows, I would like to mention a very special group of people whom I consider to be my most faithful supporters as well as my most exclusive Fan Club: the brothers "Z" – Jake and Tyler; Patrick, Jonathan, and Joseph Lavin; Daniel, Elizabeth, and Jared Sebzda; along with Grace Jonas and Samantha Claire Hobson (my little pumpkin lover). They all possess a special magic that lifts my spirit and their enthusiasm for October 31st is matched only by my own exuberance.

Lastly, but certainly not the least, a very singular and unique acknowledgement must be given to two people whom I consider my mentors when it comes to antiques and collectibles. Ladies first – to Marie Lehmann, who's been an inspiration and a true friend and teacher. You have been so generous with your time, talent, and knowledge and I've learned so much from you. I couldn't have taken on a project of this magnitude without your guidance. In the same breath, I need to acknowledge another invaluable friend and guru, Jay Forman. Your inexhaustible wealth of knowledge on the subject of antiques/collectibles is daunting and yet you always have time for my numerous questions and me. I'm glad I know you!

Introduction

In the course of conversation with fellow Halloween aficionados, a popular question is, "How long have you've been collecting?" My collection started way back when I was in grade school. It was my job to clean the family living room and dining room every Saturday and I was rewarded with a weekly allowance of twenty-five cents. I would walk to the local five-and-dime to peruse the rows of ribbons, jewelry, perfume, and seasonal goods to see how I could spend my hard-earned money. After the onslaught of September's schoolbags, pencils, rulers, and copybooks, the store would take on a golden glow with the arrival of the Halloween season. The air seemed to be perfumed with the scent of the wax red lips, fake white buckteeth, and black licorice moustaches that were sold at the counter as you entered the store. You'd walk down the aisles filled with stacks of boxed Collegeville costumes, displays of Gurley candles lined up military-fashion, and row upon row of Halloween decorations. I was able to buy a Beistle/Luhrs die-cut for a nickel and each week I added to my growing collection before Halloween was replaced with the Thanksgiving and Christmas items. I still own those autumnal decorations although they're a little worn and suffer from one-too-many tape marks.

My collecting took a serious turn in 1995 when I came across a copy of Dan and Pauline Campanelli's Halloween Collectables – A Price Guide. I guess you could say that I cut my teeth on it. This book opened up the world of vintage Halloween collectibles to me and changed the course of my collecting skills. Subsequently, I have added other guides to my library, with my latest acquisition being Mark Ledenbach's Vintage Halloween Collectibles published in 2003. This book has, in my opinion, introduced the collecting public to the rare and hard-to-find pieces that up until now only a handful of people knew existed. While poring over the pages of the book again and again, the question that nagged me was, "With the advent of this latest contribution to the Halloween-collecting community, in that it has opened up the gates to the availability to some really rare and never-before-seen items, what untapped treasures are waiting to be discovered?" Which is how this book came to be.

I'm lucky to have the good fortune of living just hours away from the Beistle Company, one of the largest manufacturers of holiday and all-occasion decorations since 1900. Knowing also that they were, and still are, one of the biggest producers of Halloween decorations since the 1920s, it wasn't a long decision-making process to see that the Beistle Company was going to factor in on my book in a big way.

Halloween collectible guides typically showcase collections belonging to several collectors, with the exception of Mark Ledenbach's whose publication is composed solely of his private collection. This guide, however, offers a twist – Beistle had the wherewithal to place an example of every item they produce in their archives for future reference. My idea was to produce a book using those items that came directly from the Beistle Company's archives. It is an absolute thrill to know that with the cooperation and permission of Beistle that I can offer this comprehensive guide for both the beginning holiday collector as well as the advanced. For the first time, collectors will be able to have the proper dating, Stock Number, and in some cases, the correct name of each Beistle Halloween creation. This is the definitive source guide for vintage Beistle Halloween collectibles.

I can't put into words the absolute exhilaration I felt every time I walked through the doors of the Beistle Company. Just anticipating the opportunity of being surrounded by the entire collection of vintage Beistle/Luhrs Halloween collectibles would be a heady experience for any collector. This far exceeded the "child in the candy store" emotion. We viewed pieces rarely seen and in some cases, were shown some that were deemed "not marketable" and were not, until this book, seen by the public.

As you can imagine, this was an exhaustive undertaking and my publisher had set certain guidelines as to the extent of quantity of information in one book. I chose to start at the beginning of their Halloween production, which in actuality was 1919 although these products were not brought to the public's attention until the 1920 Sales Catalogue. As each year progressed, the Halloween line expanded and its seasonal offerings increased accordingly. Keeping in mind that I had to "hold in the reins," this book will showcase the years from 1920 through 1949.

There is an interesting bit of information that I discovered in the course of poring over each of the yearly sales catalogues. The die-cuts that are shown with glassine envelopes were not necessarily sold as such. It seems that you had an option of buying the piece with or without an envelope/packet. So in your quest for a "complete set" (i.e., die-cut plus envelope), don't knock yourself out trying to pair up these pieces; chances are that the die-cut probably traveled solo throughout its life.

A true collector's mantra is typically, "Condition, Condition, Condition," but I sometimes have to circumvent this motto with a slightly varied rendition of, "Condition, Condition, Rarity." The old axiom, "Knowledge is power," has never been more true than when it comes to a collector. Understanding every facet of your particular collecting field will equip you in becoming a savvy negotiator. When I come upon a holiday piece that in my opinion is hard-to-find, and the decision to buy comes down to the "What am I willing to pay?" factor, I ask myself, "Will I see this again?" particularly if the asking price is out of proportion to its condition and rarity factor. To illustrate this example, recently I was bidding on a really rare Halloween die-cut from the 1920s. This particular piece wasn't in mint condition but at the very least, it was very good. I set my limit at $500.00 and hoped that my bid would come in at the low 400s. Needless to say, the auction ended with the High Bidder getting the item for almost $950.00! In my opinion when an auction such as this nets an extreme amount, it doesn't take much time before these pieces are being pulled from boxes, storage, and personal collections and put up for sale. I'm a very patient person, so I'll wait. But most importantly, the one creed I do live by when I come across some fantastic Halloween piece that has dubious provenance, "When in doubt, do without!"

Photographically, it is much more interesting to group similar items in one shot as it makes for a more provocative subject matter. However, I felt that each Beistle Halloween piece deserved its own "limelight," if you will. Showcasing each article will enable you to give it your undivided attention to study the particular nuance of each piece.

Each caption will have at least one corresponding photo to go along with the legend. In the case of sets (i.e., set of 4, set of 12, etc.) and/or multi-sided lanterns, the number of photos will increase accordingly.

Each description will begin with the Beistle-assigned name in bold type. The Original Stock Number and the Initial Year the item was released follows. The italicized paragraphs are those taken directly from the yearly Beistle Sales Catalogues. Any comments made by me will be preceded with an asterisk (*). Lastly, I have assigned a value to each piece and/or set, which will be in bold type as the last line of each description.

A Brief History of the Beistle Company

The Beistle Company was founded in 1900, in Pittsburgh, Pennsylvania, by Martin Luther Beistle, in the basement of his home. A company with such small beginnings has grown over the past 100 years to become one of today's largest American Halloween party novelty manufacturers. Originally from Walnut Bottom, Pennsylvania, "ML" decided to move to "the city" to pursue a career. To supplement his income as a calendar salesman, ML started to craft décor for hotel and theatre lobbies. He subsequently moved the Beistle Company back to his wife's hometown of Oakville, and, in 1908, the business relocated to larger facilities in Shippensburg, Pennsylvania.

Soon after relocating, the Company expanded its product line to include wooden toys, games, and paper seasonal decorations primarily for the Christmas holiday. In 1917, after patenting a method for honeycombed tissue production, Beistle turned its primary concentration to the manufacture of printed and tissue paper products, which would become the Company's distinguishing feature. It was at this time that Halloween decorations were added to the line. In the mid-1920s, Valentine and Easter products were introduced.

The United States entry into World War II brought with it a shortage of the Company's ordinary raw material and a resurgence of patriotism. During this time Beistle shifted its manufacturing to the production of human and bomb parachutes, and watertight shipment wrapping. For its contribution to the war effort, Beistle was awarded the "E" for excellence by the Federal War Department.

After the war, Beistle once again started production of paper novelties, this time adding printed paper and foil New Year's and everyday products. The 1960s saw the addition of thermo-formed plastic hats. Throughout its history, The Beistle Company product line has continually expanded and diversified to meet the demands of the customers.

The Beistle Company has been a true "family business." In its more than 100 years of business, five generations of M.L. Beistle's descendents have led the Company to exceptional growth and success. Many generations of area families also have worked at the Company, thus giving a true meaning to the phrase The Beistle Family. This family tradition both strengthens and propels the Company into the future. This means that a collector can look forward to finding quality Beistle products for many years to come.

This book is a wonderful documentation of the rich history of Beistle's early production of Halloween paper party goods and decorations. Claire Lavin has spent many hours tirelessly documenting a portion of our vast archives. Through her efforts this book has been brought to fruition and its existence will facilitate the collector of vintage Halloween decorations in their efforts to identify and value their collectibles.

Terriann L. Hilbinger
Great-granddaughter of M.L. Beistle

Using the Value Guide

The values listed represent, in the opinion of the author, what an item (which is in excellent condition) might be valued at by the educated collector. The pieces illustrated are priced as excellent. The price paid for any particular article will, naturally, vary by geographical location and will also be affected by the buyer's enthusiasm, the disposition of the seller, and where the item is purchased (i.e. an antique show, retail shop, flea market, etc.)

Rare or desirable items in excellent or mint condition, which may include original packaging (box, bag, wrapper, etc.) can, in some instances, be worth several times the values suggested.

In the end, the price paid for any particular piece depends on the buyer and seller. The author does not claim to be the final authority on prices and, therefore, the publisher and/or the author assume no responsibility for financial loss or gain based on the use of this guide.

Opposite page: Graphic design by Bob Hansen.

October's Party
by George Cooper

Back when I attended grade school, part of our curriculum was to memorize poetry. In third grade one of the first poems assigned was "October's Party" by George Cooper. This piece has always conjured up the look and feel of what I consider the most wonderful time of the year. It boggles my mind that I can still recite the first stanza from memory and it's been over 40 years since my parochial school days. It has remained my all-time favorite narrative to this day. I've included this work at the beginning of the book and then with a bit of "poetic license" have put a new twist on its theme in keeping with the subject of my book. My sincere apologies to George Cooper.

I've also borrowed one stanza from John Greenleaf Whittier's poem "The Pumpkin." It seemed fitting to include this piece since my first choice in Halloween collectibles is the Jack-O-Lantern.

October gave a party;
The leaves by hundreds came –
The Chestnuts, Oaks and Maples,
And leaves of every name.
The Sunshine spread a carpet,
And everything was grand,
Miss Weather led the dancing,
Professor Wind the band.

The Chestnuts came in yellow,
The Oaks in crimson dressed;
The lovely Misses Maple
In scarlet looked their best;
All balanced to their partners,
And gaily fluttered by;
The sight was like a rainbow
New fallen from the sky.

Then, in the rustic hollow,
At hide-and-seek they played,
The party closed at sundown,
And everybody stayed.
Professor Wind played louder;
They flew along the ground;
And then the party ended
In jolly "hands around."

CHAPTER I

YOU ARE INVITED... INVITATIONS

"October gave a party,
The pleas by dozens came... "

HALLOWEEN FOLDING INVITATIONS
Original Stock No. 1002
Initial Release: 1925
Size 2" x 2.25", printed in orange and black with invitations on the inside, die-cut, six in envelope.
*Two views of invitations shown here.
Value: $85.00

NOVELTY "HARK EERIE WAILINGS" FOLDING HALLOWEEN INVITATION
Original Stock No. 838
Initial Release: 1930
One design, ghost with folded arms rising from Jack-O-'Lantern, arms unfold robe to reveal face and invitation, each with white mailing envelope 4.5" x 6-5/8".
Value: $45.00

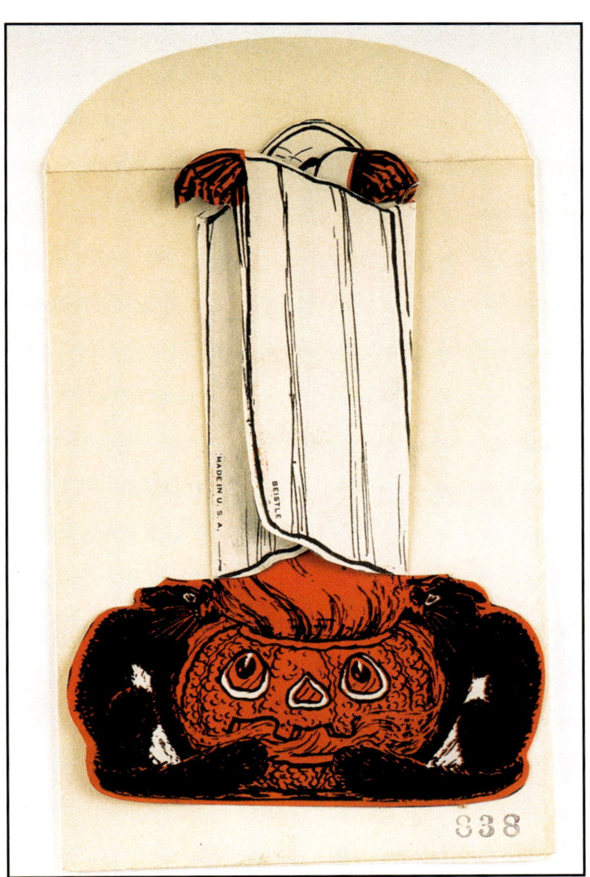

MECHANICAL HALLOWEEN INVITATION
Original Stock No. 833
Initial Release: 1932
One design, Grandfather Clock, door opens to reveal invitation, mechanical figures, hidden behind clock, each with white mailing envelope, 3.25" x 7.75".
Value: $75.00

NOVELTY HALLOWEEN INVITATION

Original Stock No. 1021
Initial Release: 1928
When the invitation is opened, the old witch rises up in front on the inside. Size when folded 3" x 4.5", each with an envelope.
Value: $75.00

NOVELTY FOLDING INVITATION

Original Stock No. 837
Initial Release: 1930
One design – rustic fence and patch of Jack-O-Lanterns with moon that rises when unfolded revealing invitation. Each with white mailing envelope 3.75" x 5.5".
Value: $65.00

MECHANICAL INVITATION
Original Stock No. 834
Initial Release: 1930
One design, garden gate with black cat and rising moon, invitation revealed as moon rises. Each with white mailing envelope 5.375" x 5.75".
Value: $75.00

MECHANICAL INVITATION
Original Stock No. 835
Initial Release: 1930
One design, Halloween Jack-O-Lantern, moveable tongue and eyes with fluttering bat having mechanical wings. Invitation printed on tongue. Each with white mailing envelope 5.375" x 5.75".
Value: $75.00

NOVELTY FOLDING INVITATION
Original Stock No. 836
Initial Release: 1932
Printed on folding stock, each with white mailing envelope measuring 3" x 4.5".
*Showing packaged invitations along with some examples with a sheet of uncut invitations as a backdrop.
Value: $75.00

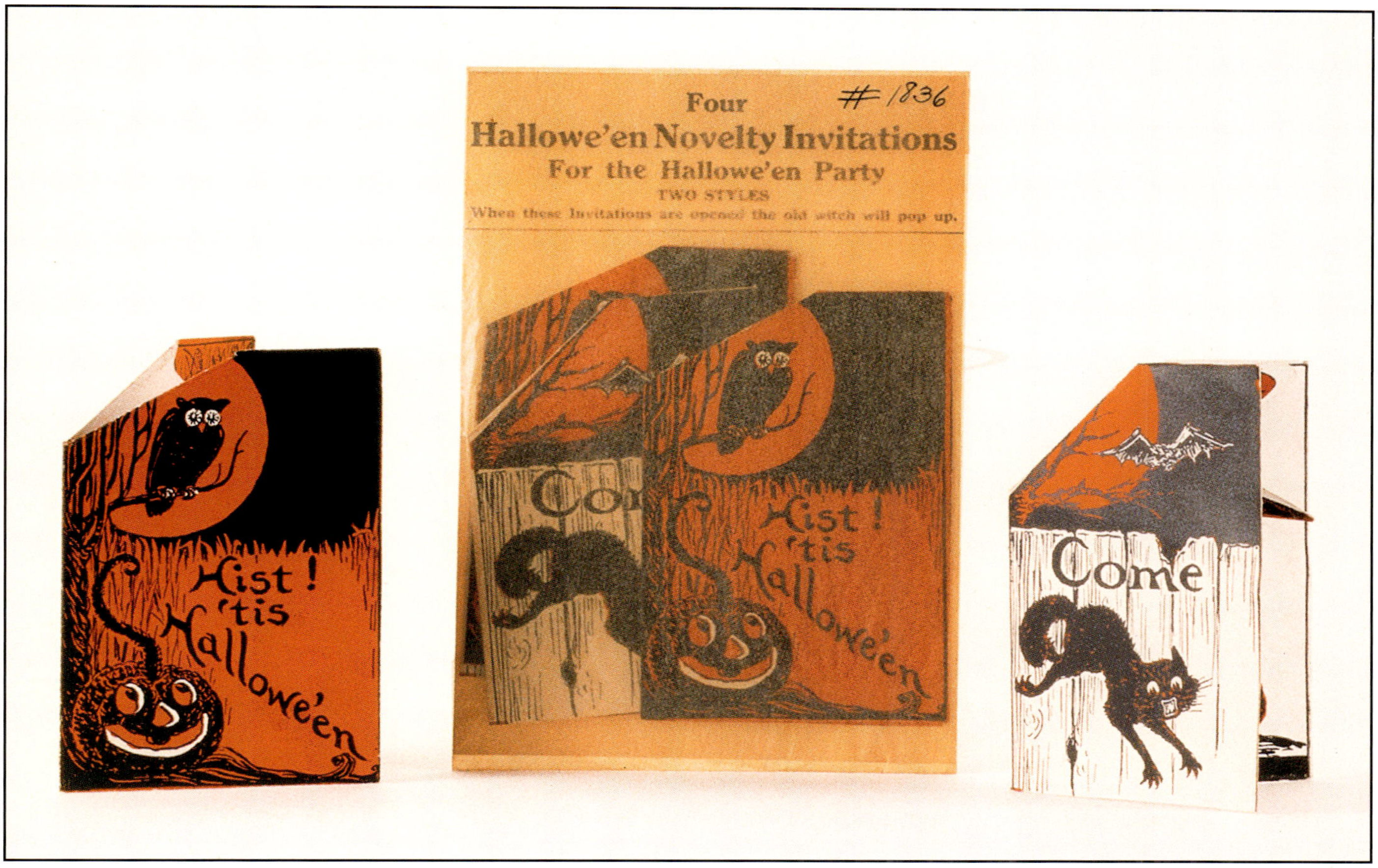

Four
Hallowe'en Novelty Invitations
For the Hallowe'en Party
TWO STYLES
When these Invitations are opened the old witch will pop up.

#1836

Hist! 'tis Hallowe'en

Come

CHAPTER II

PARTY HELPS

"The Place Cards, Tallies and Nut Cups,
And Party Helps of every name..."

MAK-UR-OWN PARTY SIGNS
Original Stock No. 1899
Initial Release: 1948
Use for fun and utility. Assorted four appropriate designs in three colors on cardboard. Blank space for making signs, directions, or funny sayings. Suggestions for use on back of each. Each measures 9" x 12.5".
Value: $115.00 each

HALLOWE'EN SIGNS

(Letter Your Own)

Add a distinctive and personal note for your Hallowe'en Party by using these attractively designed signs. There is no end to the variety of originality and individuality you can display in the use of these clever decorations. They have been particularly planned to include a note of utility and practicability.

Use crayon, soft pencil or paint with ink and simply write or letter directions or slogans to amuse or create hilarious party spirit or atmosphere.

SOME SUGGESTED USES: Create "spooky" feelings, or jolly Hallowe'en spirits for party fun. Give directions at your parties, and dances in the home, school or organization entertainments. Use simply as a decoration with your own clever sayings. Use for store window decorations by adding special notices, sales prices, or other eye-catching holiday matters. Attract attention by using on merchandise or other counter displays. Direct customers to items on special sale, or to other Hallowe'en bargains.

There are four different designs available, buy all four to have variety.

Made in U. S. A. | A Beistle Creation | No. 1899

HALLOWEEN FAVOR BASKETS
Original Stock No. 631
Initial Release: 1928
Three styles measuring 4" in diameter and 3" high, three assorted in transparent bag.
*Only two of the three styles were available from the Beistle archives.
Value: $225.00

NUT CUP TRANSPARENCY
Original Stock No. 1140
Initial Release: 1941
Halloween silhouette nut cups cut from two-toned orange and black paper with green transparency. Fold to shape. Each measuring 2.5" x 3.25".
Value: $85.00

NUT CUPS AND CANDY TRAYS
Original Stock No. 865
Initial Release: 1932
Assorted two designs, size 3.5" x 3.5", with a 1.25" cup at the base. Printed orange and black on white folding stock, both sides, and reversible so as to give two designs. Sides of the cup at the base fold and hook together with a novel joint, space for place card arranged.
Value: $65.00

PARTY OUTFIT IN ENVELOPE
Original Stock No. 2579
Initial Release: 1925
Halloween Party Outfit in an envelope size 6.75" x 11.25", in full colors for a party of four. Each assortment contains 30 pieces: lampshades, candleholders, invitations, place cards, nut cups and ice cream decorations. All printed in bright Halloween colors, die-cut ready to pull out and set up – no pasting required – together with "Helps and Stunts" for a Halloween Party.
*Making its debut in 1925, the Party Kit was offered to the consumer in a choice of box or beautifully decorated envelope. In the 1927 sales catalogue, the kit was offered in an envelope or simply as a booklet. In 1928, the booklet came in two sizes – 6" x 11" sold in an envelope whereas the 7" x 11.75" model sold as is. The 7" x 11.75" booklet was the only model offered in 1929 whereas the 6" x 11" booklet was the sole offering for 1930. This included the envelope. Both pieces returned in the 1931 and 1932 sales catalogues and then reverted back to the 7" x 11" book for 1933, where it ended its run of nine years.
Value: $450.00

HALLOWEEN TICKLERS
Stock No. 66
Initial Release: 1928
Measuring 22" long with 12" heavy paper handle. Designs printed on both sides in bright Halloween colors.
*Due to the fragility of this piece, I doubt many survived.
Value: $225.00

PARTY STUNTS
Original Stock No. 629
Initial Release: 1928
Sixteen cards size 2.5" x 3" with round corners, each with a different stunt for a Halloween party. Packaged in an envelope with cellophane opening. Size of envelope 4" x 5.5" in bright orange and black front.
Value: $65.00

TALLY AND SCORE CARD SETS
Original Stock No. 864
Initial Release: 1932
Assorted two designs measuring 3.5" x 5". Printed on white paper with movable overalls or apron stitched to front covering place to keep score. Each piece decorated with an orange cord and silk tassel. "Five Hundred" and "Bridge" printed on back.
Value: $50.00 set

FORTUNE PLACE CARDS
Original Stock No. 756
Initial Release: 1928
Shape of hat with fortunes tucked in at the top. Five place cards and five fortunes contained in package.
Value: $65.00

HALLOWEEN JACK-O-LANTERN DECORATION
Original Stock No. 1017
Initial Release: 1925
Ten assorted Pumpkins size about 3" x 3", in Halloween colors and die-cut. This package is made up so that Pumpkins can be used as a decoration or they can be used as a Pumpkin Fortune Game, as each Pumpkin has a Fortune on the back for a boy or girl with full instructions how to use them, making a double value.
Value: $85.00

HALLOWEEN PUMPKIN HEAD FAVORS
Original Stock No. 1009
Initial Release: 1925
Size 5" x 2.25", with easel support, printed in Halloween colors and die-cut, five in envelope.
**In the 1930 catalogue, the Stock Number for this item changes to No. 514.*
Value: $85.00

CAT HEAD SEALS
Original Stock No. 760C
Initial Release: 1931
Assorted three designs Cat Heads, size 2.25" in diameter, printed in Halloween colors, gummed back, packed nine pieces in a printed envelope 4.5" x 5.25".
Value: $85.00

GUMMED PUMPKIN DECORATIONS
Original Stock No. 1054
Initial Release: 1924
Seven designs in black and orange on glazed stock size 3" x 3". Twelve pieces to an envelope.
*Stock Number 1054 changed to Number 1055 in later years.
Value: $45.00

ROCKER FAVORS
Original Stock No. 760R
Initial Release: 1931
Assorted six designs, size 3" x 3.25", printed in colors and die-cut. Six pieces to an envelope.
Value: $45.00

MECHANICAL PLACE CARDS
Original Stock No. 757
Initial Release: 1930
Assorted four designs, size 2.5" x 2.75", movable cover for a nameplate attached with eyelet. Four pieces to an envelope.
Value: $65.00

AUTUMN LEAVES
Original Stock No. 746
Initial Release: 1930
One design, natural colored printed Autumn Leaves, die-cut, size 4" x 4.25". Twelve pieces to an envelope.
Value: $45.00

HALLOWEEN SEALS
Original Stock No. 760H
Initial Release: 1925
Assorted thirty-five pieces printed in Halloween colors with gummed back die-cut, complete in a printed envelope 4.5" x 5.25".
*This item was first marketed under Stock No. 1020 and then changed to No. 760H. It appears that No. 1020 came with the instruction sheet, "How to decorate with Halloween Seals" whereas there is no mention of this on No. 760H.
Value: $65.00

HALLOWEEN NUT OR CANDY TRAYS
Original Stock No. 760N
Initial Release: 1931
Packed four assorted designs in a printed envelope.
Value: $65.00

MECHANICAL NUT CUPS
Original Stock No. 1055
Initial Release: 1938
Answers the sales question, "We want something different" and you can give them a mechanical nut cup printed and die-cut on cardboard, folds flat, size 3" x 4.5" average. Four different designs to a set.
Value: $85.00 set

FLAMING FORTUNE DECORATIONS
Original Stock No. 901
Initial Release: 1929
One design, 7", orange honeycomb tissue base, forms part of Candle Holder Centerpiece, in which is set a printed flaming candle, six flames of which are removable, each with a different fortune. All packed in a printed folding box.
*In 1931, Beistle reissued this game/centerpiece with two changes: twelve flame fortunes in place of the original six and the later version was packed in a printed transparent envelope in lieu of the folding box.
Value: $ 900.00 (for either version)

SILHOUETTES
Original Stock No. 1056
Initial Release: 1933
Assorted eighteen kinds average size 4", die-cut Halloween characters in sheet form on black stock with gummed back, and with waste stock pulled out, folded, with a white card size 5" x 6.75", showing in reduced size the contents, and with directions for use. Packed in a glassine bag 5" x 7".
Stock No. 1050
Same as the above set but the material is heavy album stock and the back is not gummed (glued).
*In the 1940 catalogue, the display card featured a black cat silhouette. This was the only noticeable change. (Photo shows both display cards)
Value: $75.00

SILHOUETTES
Original Stock No. 573
Initial Release: 1929
Twenty-five assorted, fine detail, cut from heavy black stock, packed in sliding cover box 5.5" x 7" x .5". Box printed in Halloween colors with suggestions for use printed on back.
Value: $115.00

SILHOUETTES
Original Stock No. 1050
Initial Release: 1933
Assorted eighteen kinds of average size 4", die cut Halloween characters in sheet form on heavy album stock with the waste stock pulled out, folded, with a card size 5" x 6.75". Showing in reduced size the contents, and with directions for used. Packed in a glassine bag 5" x 7".
Value: $85.00

SMALL ROLY POLYS
Original Stock No. 692P
Initial Release: 1930
Assorted four designs, printed on cardboard both sides, in full Halloween colors. Stand 8" high and with heavy weighted honeycomb tissue ball bottom, 5" in diameter.
*These Roly Polys differ from Stock No. 692 in that they have an added tissue paper plume attached at the top, hence the "P" at the end of the Stock Number. Although there are four designs, I could only find three of them in the Beistle archives.
Value: $175.00 each

HALLOWEEN STANDING DECORATIONS
Original Stock No. 1624
Initial Release: 1925
Six assorted pumpkins and silhouettes ranging in size from 6.5" x 3.75" to 4.75" x 8.5" complete with easel supports. Packed six assorted in an attractively printed envelope which measures 6.75" x 11.5".
Value: $145.00

CAKE AND FRUIT DECORATIONS
Original Stock No. 640
Initial Release: 1920
Printed on heavy stock on both sides measuring 1.75" x 4.75", twelve assorted designs in package.
*Beistle discontinued this item after only three years, probably due to lack of interest. Interestingly, the Dennison Company had numerous variations in their version of this type of pick. Also, they printed fortunes on the back for additional sales "oomph."
Value: $145.00

HALLOWEEN PLACE CARDS
Original Stock No. 584
Initial Release: 1920
Three designs in orange and black on glazed stock, die-cut and measuring 3" x 4.25". To be suspended from the edge of a drinking glass.
Value: $65.00 each

HALLOWEEN COSTUME FRINGE
Original Stock No. 77
Initial Release: 1927
Ten separate pieces of shredded orange colored honey comb tissue paper. Each fringe expands 14" long and is 11.5" deep. Each set of ten pieces is in a bag with design printed on front showing "How to decorate a costume."
Value: $55.00

MECHANICAL FIGURE PLACE CARDS
Original Stock No. 847
Initial Release: 1930
Assorted four designs printed on heavy stock. Average size is 3.25" x 4.5". Figures die-cut with arms and legs attached with brass fasteners so they can be moved. Equipped with an easel back.
*The four assorted designs include two Pumpkin Dolls, one Harlequin and one Witch.
Value: $115.00 each

NOVELTY PLACE CARDS
Original Stock No. 846
Initial Release: 1932
Four assorted designs printed on white stock embossed each with verse. Each fitted with a novelty patented Jack-O-Lantern support that swings open ready to stand.
Value: $55.00

RATTLE
Original Stock No. 1189
Initial Release: 1933
Assorted four designs printed in orange and black and varnished on cardboard stock, die-cut and folded to make a box in which is inserted a wooden handle with attached orange tissue plumes.
*It appears that you could fill the box with either dried beans or rice to really enhance the sound of the rattle. All four designs shown here with the Owl figure fully assembled.
Value: $145.00 each

CARDBOARD NOISE MAKERS
Original Stock No. 1763
Initial Release: 1939
You'll be SURPRISED at the cardboard noisemakers that slip into your pocket flat!
*What a wonderful discovery I made! Three patterns as shown in the photo. Too bad these only lasted one season – I guess they weren't popular with the public.
Value: $95.00 each

WALL DECORATION
Original Stock No. 1133
Initial Release: 1933
One design, six fighting Halloween black cats, printed black and orange on heavy cardboard, varnished and die-cut in six 12" panels, making a decoration 6' long. Each panel is eyeletted together and with eyelet reinforcements at the ends for string hanger. Each cat has tail eyeletted and is moveable. Card illustrating decoration and uses is attached to back.
Value: $145.00

CAT HEAD STREAMER
Original Stock No. 1126
Initial Release: 1933
One design, fifteen cats printed black on tangerine stock, die-cut and fastened at regular intervals on a 9' string, making a big wall decoration. Each streamer packed in a glassine bag.
*Recognize the Cat Head? It's taken from the 1931 Beistle die-cut "Skairo – The Halloween Bug."
Value: $75.00

HALLOWEEN PENNANT DECORATION
Original Stock No. 851
Initial Release: 1920
Fourteen pennants, all different Halloween designs printed in orange and black on semi-transparent paper attached to string 6' long, 11" drop.
Value: $135.00

WALL DECORATION
Original Stock No. 1649
Initial Release: 1936
Popular big value! Silhouettes on a 5' wall decoration, printed black and orange on folding panels of cardboard.
*This item was offered with or without a glassine bag with display card.
Value: $75.00 (with or without bag)

CAT FACE BANNER
Original Stock No. 1850
Initial Release: 1948
The large cat faces create party spirit. Printed in black on heavy cardboard and eyeletted together to form a banner 50" long. Size of each cat face 6" x 7". One design.
*This item was offered with or without a glassine bag with a large illustrated, descriptive card. In 1949, Beistle offered this garland in orange and black (as seen in the photo).
Value: $65.00 (with or without bag)

HALLOWEEN BANNER
Original Stock No. 1653
Initial Release: 1937
Different Halloween designs printed in orange and black on orange tissue paper on folding panels. Measures 5' long.
Value: $85.00

SILHOUETTE CUT OUT GARLAND
Original Stock No. 1748
Initial Release: 1938
An unusually attractive silhouette garland, die cut characters on folding panels, 5' in length.
Value: $75.00

JACK-O-LANTERN GARLAND
Original Stock No. 1746
Initial Release: 1938
A brilliant array of orange Jack-O-Lanterns on printed cardboard with folding panels forming a 5' spread.
Value: $85.00

HALLOWEEN PUMPKIN SPANGLES
Original Stock No. 76
Initial Release: 1928
Six assorted faces, measuring 3.25" x 6.75" in diameter. All printed in bright Halloween colors on both sides and die-cut. Each Spangle is suspended on a 12" tape and the set is tied together with a printed tag, "How to decorate a Costume."
Value: $135.00

TALLY AND SCORE CARD SET
Original Stock No. 863
Initial Release: 1929
Assorted two designs, 2.375" x 5", printed on heavy folding stock, "Five Hundred" and "Bridge" scores printed on inside.
Value: $45.00 each

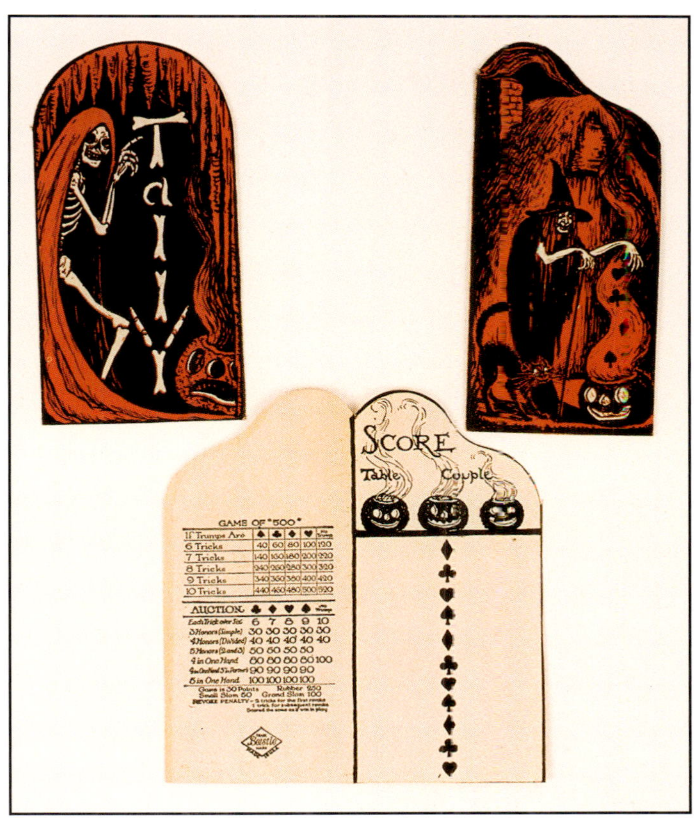

NUT CUPS AND CANDY TRAYS
Original Stock No. 866
Initial Release: 1929
Assorted three designs or styles, measuring 3.5" x 6", printed on heavy white folding paper, die-cut, complete in printed sliding cover box. Box measures 5.5" x 7" x .5" with directions for setting up printed on back.
*Of the three designs featured in this boxed set, I could only find these two Halloween Fairy examples in the archives (the other pieces can be found as Stock Number 865 first introduced in 1932). As such, the value is for a single Halloween Fairy nut cup. To have all three designs as well as the box would hold a much higher value.
Value: $95.00 each

CAT CENTERPIECE
Original Stock No. 1982
Initial Release: 1949
An attractive centerpiece – a sitting, winking cat printed on both sides in black on heavy cardboard. Full opening 6" orange mesh tissue base. Cat measures 12" tall. One design.
*The cat centerpiece on the right with the green mesh tissue base was just used as a mock-up but was not offered in this color as of 1949.
Value: $110.00

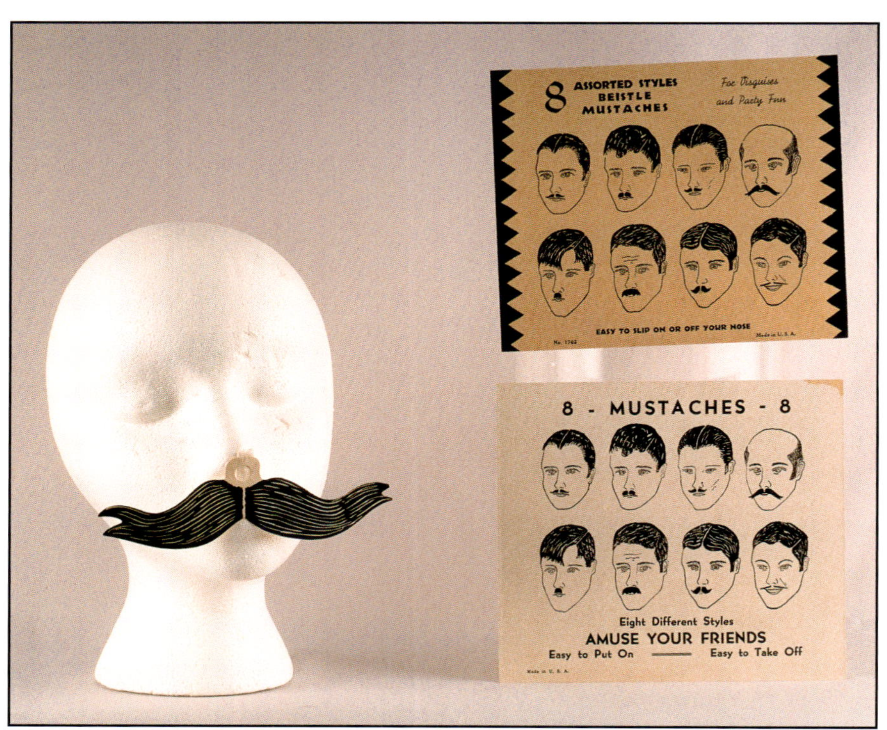

MUSTACHES
Original Stock No. 1362
Initial Release: 1936
Eight designs printed on cardboard with nose holder.
Value: $35.00 for complete set with illustrated description card

CAT SILHOUETTES
Original Stock No. 760S
Initial Release: 1932
One design, size 3.5" x 4.25", die cut from black album stock. Packed six pieces in a printed envelope.
Value: $65.00

WITCHES WITH TISSUE SKIRTS
Original Stock No. 610
Initial Release: 1930
One design, assorted six color combinations for tissue skirt. Halloween Witch printed in colors on cardboard standing 14.5" high, 8.5" wide, with jointed arms eyeletted to body and with a wide bright colored honeycomb tissue skirt. Colors of skirt orange, black, green, yellow, orange and green, and yellow and black. Each with an easel on back.
*The girls are modeling the orange and green and the black skirt respectively.
Value: $150.00 each

CHAPTER III
DIE-CUTS

"The Hostess wove her magic,
And everything was grand..."

SKELETON JUMPING JACKS
Original Stock No. 1140
Initial Release: 1930
One design, 18" high, printed orange and black on cardboard and die-cut with all joints eyeletted. Fitted with string hangers and string harness on the back, which gives jumping action when pulled.
Value: $125.00

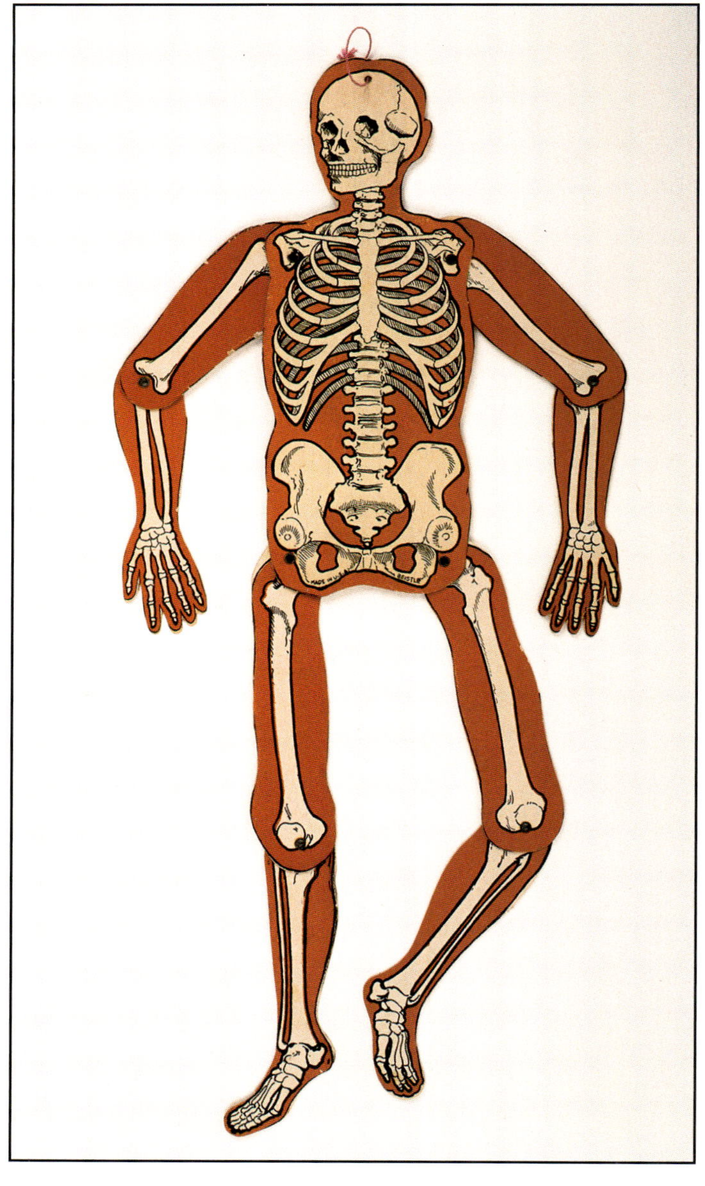

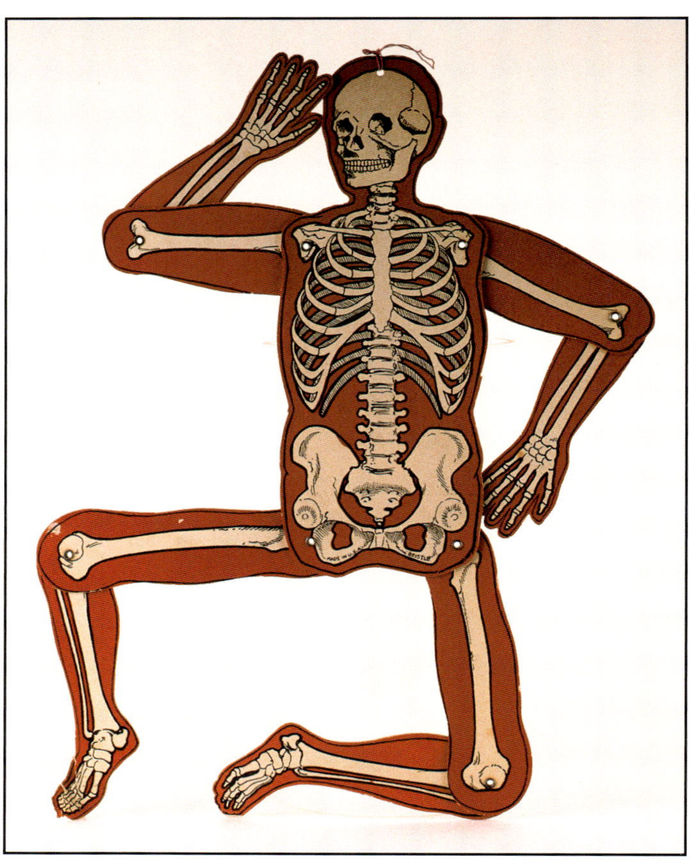

JACK-O-LANTERN DECORATIONS
Original Stock No. 586
Initial Release: 1930
Assorted two designs, average size 7", printed one side on cardboard, 3" novelty pedestal which swings open ready to stand.
Value: $110.00/set

SKULL DECORATIONS
Original Stock No. 595
Initial Release: 1932
Assorted two designs, average size 6.5", printed one side on cardboard, 3" novelty pedestal which swings open to stand for a base.
Value: $110.00/set

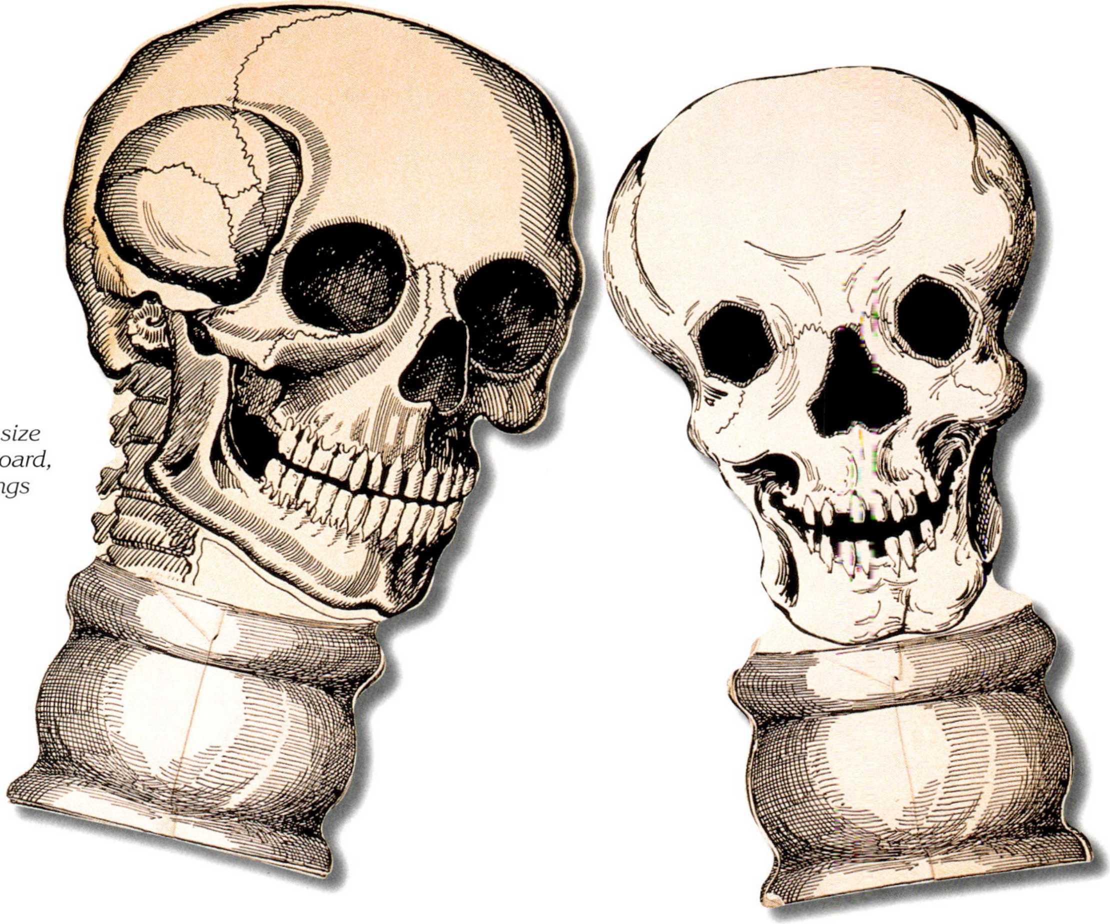

OLD WITCH
Original Stock No. 1149
Initial Release: 1925
Halloween Dancing Witch, 18" high, in full Halloween colors, with string harness on the back. Pull the string and see the wings and arms jump. It is very amusing as well as decorative. Size when open 18" x 18.5."
*This Halloween Witch got two billings in the 1925 catalogue. Along with the above, she was assigned another Stock Number of 1648. The only difference between the two is that #1648 came in an attractively printed envelope. In later years, this die-cut's Stock Number changed to #648 and #2648 respectively. The variance in Stock Numbers is the result of the item's quantity changing from year to year (i.e., 1925 = three dozen in a box, 1927 = dozen to a box, 1928 = dozen to a box).
Value: $225.00

SKELETON
Original Stock No. 2643
Initial Release: 1927
2-sided Jointed Skeleton measuring 25" x 37" packaged in a glassine envelope.
Value: $55.00

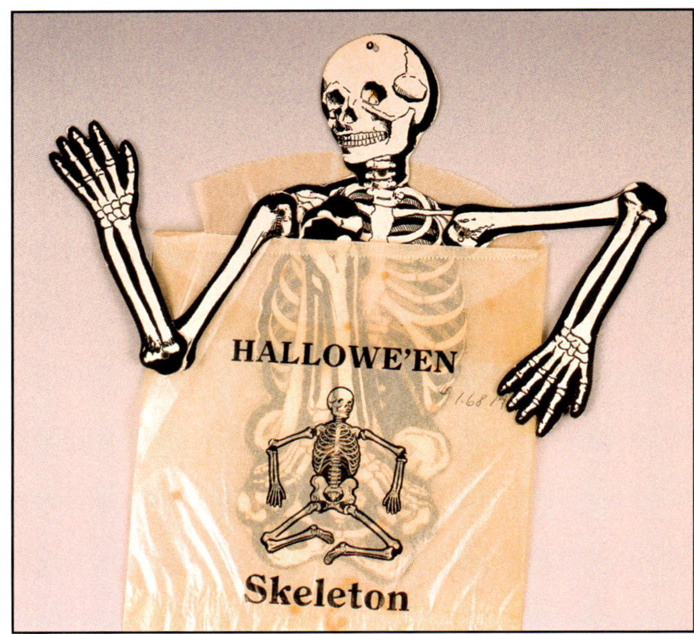

"LIGHTNING WUMPUS"
Original Stock No. 698X
Initial Release: 1931
One design, "The Halloween Devil", 30" high, printed orange and black on cardboard, die-cut, with thirteen eyeletted joints, and with an orange string hanger.
*This piece was sold with or without a printed transparent bag; the Stock Number #698 was given to the piece that included the bag.
Value: $425.00

"SKAIRO"
Original Stock No. 697
Initial Release: 1929
"The Halloween Bug" measures 29" high and is printed orange and black on cardboard, die-cut, with thirteen eyeletted joints, and with an orange string hanger. Each packed in a printed transparent bag.
Value: $425.00

"SKAIRO"
Original Stock No. 697X
Initial Release: 1931
One design, "The Halloween Bug" measures 29" high, printed orange and black on cardboard, die-cut, with thirteen eyeletted joints and with an orange string hanger.
*Stock Number 697 featured the above die-cut with a printed transparent bag.
Value: $425.00

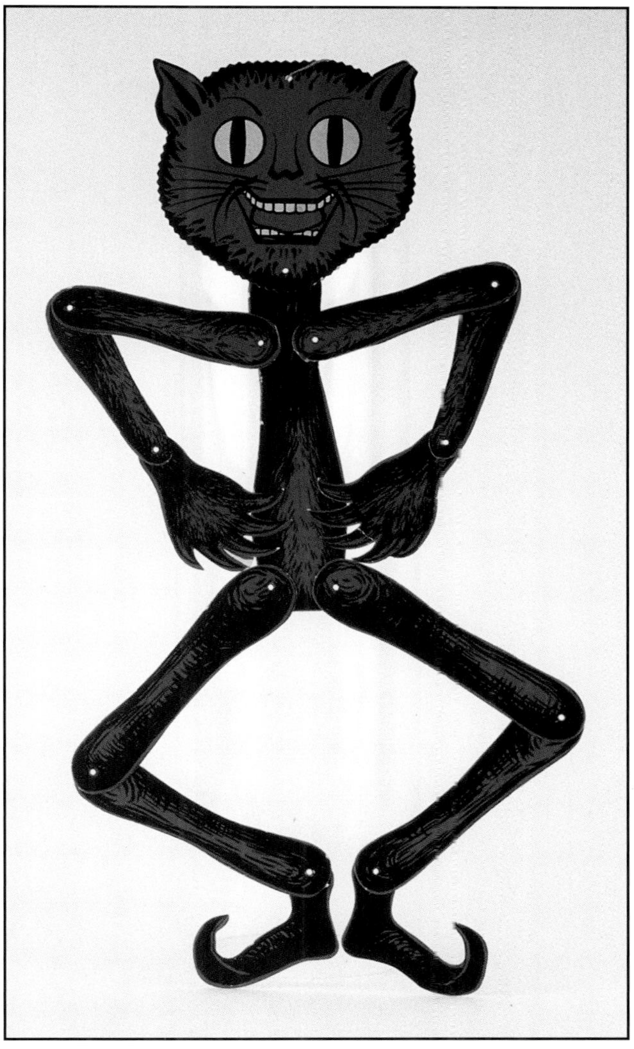

"LIGHTNING WUMPUS"
Original Stock No. 698
Initial Release: 1929
"The Halloween Dragon" measures 30" high, printed orange and black on cardboard, die-cut, with thirteen jointed eyeletted joints and with an orange string hanger. Each in a printed transparent bag.
Value: $425.00

EMBOSSED HALLOWEEN FIGURES
Original Stock No. 1552
Initial Release: 1933
Twelve designs measuring 8" x 9". Attractive Halloween designs of Cats, Witches, Owls, etc., in humorous poses, printed in bright colors, embossed, and die-cut, and with a hole at top of design for hanging.
*For some inexplicable reason, the archive's set is missing the Winking Owl and Quarter-Moon die cut.
Value: $75.00-135.00 range
(Continued on following pages)

GO
STOP
DETOUR

A COMPLETE HALLOWEEN DECORATION ASSORTMENT
Original Stock No. 1122
Initial Release: 1941*
Twelve different cardboard cutouts for wall or window decoration use. The designs are printed in five assorted colors. Four large subjects about 12" x 22"; eight small subjects 10" x 12". Packed 12 assorted in a printed envelope.
*These 12 designs were initially released in 1938 but were broken down into two sets; the eight smaller die-cuts were listed as Stock No. 1340 while the remaining four larger decorations were listed under Stock No. 1345. Not surprisingly, these 12 assorted die-cuts were grouped and packaged in various configurations and naturally were given new Stock Numbers. Additionally, they can be found under Stock Nos. 1119, 1120, 1617, and 1619 respectively.
Value: $425.00
(Continued on following pages)

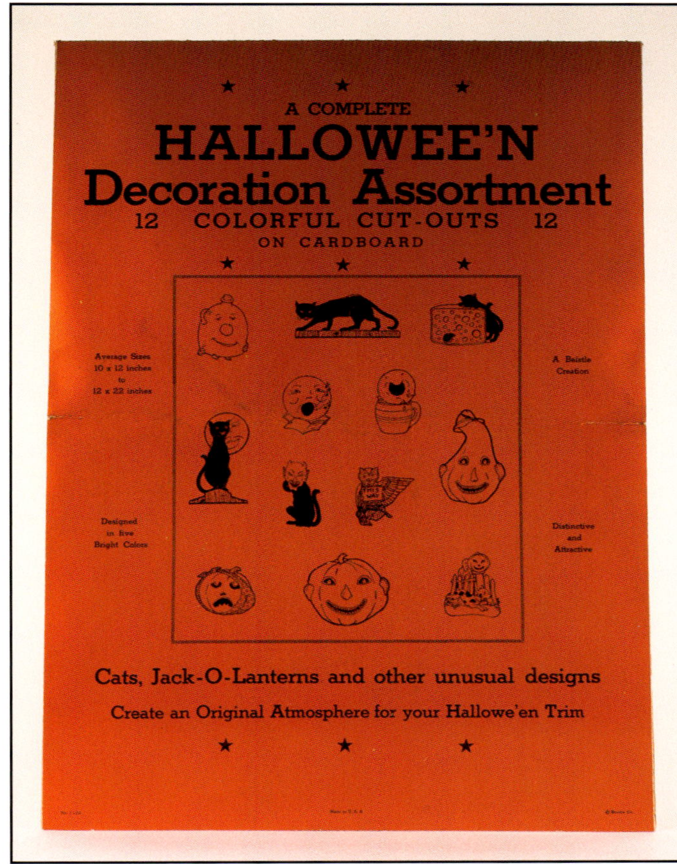

THIS
WAY

HALLOWEEN JUMPING JACKS

Original Stock No. 1139-1144
Initial Release: 1925

Four kinds: skeleton (two sizes – 18-1/3" & 23"), clown (two sizes – 15" & 19"), devil (17" named Old Nick), and veggie man (19.5" named Halloween Dancing Elf), all in Halloween colors with eyelet joints and string hangers, each with string harness on the back.

*The devil is featured here. The skeleton was featured as a separate item in the 1925 catalogue and was given the Stock No. 1140 and 1143 (for the 18.5" and 23" respectively) and Old Nick was assigned Stock No. 1144. The clown, devil, and skeleton were combined under the Stock No. 1143 in the 1928 catalogue and the skeleton and devil resurfaced as a duo in the 1931 catalogue and were sold under the same Stock No. 1143.

Value: $135.00-155.00

WITCH DECORATION

Stock No. 1136
Initial Release: 1933

One design, new type walking witch with head, hands and feet printed in full colors and varnished, and die-cut, size 15" x 23". The figure is attached to sheet of heavy chipboard for protection in shipping.

*In the same catalogue there is a variation to this die-cut listed under Stock No. 1135. Instead of the die-cut being made of one large piece of cardboard, the dress and shawl were made of cloth print beifoli tissue paper die-cut and mounted in place (see photo). Again, this same witch was given the Stock No. 1137 in the 1934-35 catalogue and apparently Beistle decided to forego stitching the piece to a board as previously mentioned in the 1933 catalogue. Note another interpretation of tissue paper adornment to this die-cut from one of Beistle's artists (see second photo). This latter piece was never released to the public.

This wonderfully detailed Witch had quite a long run. Making her debut in 1933, her popularity lasted at least up until 1949, the year I stopped covering in this book. Can you pick out the subtle variations in each of these die-cuts?

VALUE: $225.00-375.00

(Continued on following pages)

15 X 23 5/8

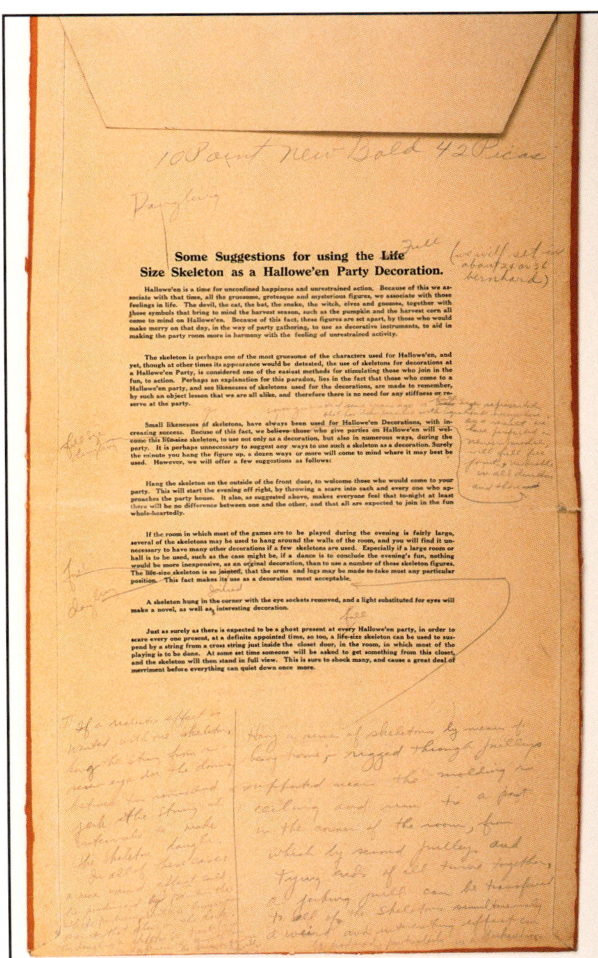

Some Suggestions for using the Life Size Skeleton as a Hallowe'en Party Decoration.

Hallowe'en is a time for unconfined happiness and unrestrained action. Because of this we associate with that time, all the gruesome, grotesque and mysterious figures, we associate with those feelings in life. The devil, the cat, the bat, the snake, the witch, elves and gnomes, together with those symbols that bring to mind the harvest season, such as the pumpkin and the harvest corn all come to mind on Hallowe'en. Because of this fact, these figures are set apart, by those who would make merry on that day, in the way of party gathering, to use as decorative instruments, to aid in making the party room more in harmony with the feeling of unrestrained activity.

The skeleton is perhaps one of the most gruesome of the characters used for Hallowe'en, and yet, though at other times its appearance would be detested, the use of skeletons for decorations at a Hallowe'en Party, is considered one of the easiest methods for stimulating those who join in the fun, to action. Perhaps an explanation for this paradox, lies in the fact that those who come to a Hallowe'en party, and see likenesses of skeletons used for the decorations, are made to remember, by such an object lesson that we are all alike, and therefore there is no need for any stiffness or reserve at the party.

Small likenesses of skeletons, have always been used for Hallowe'en Decorations, with increasing success. Becuse of this fact, we believe those who give parties on Hallowe'en will welcome this lifesize skeleton, to use not only as a decoration, but also in numerous ways, during the party. It is perhaps unnecessary to suggest any ways to use such a skeleton as a decoration. Surely the minute you hang the figure up, a dozen ways or more will come to mind where it may best be used. However, we will offer a few suggestions as follows:

Hang the skeleton on the outside of the front door, to welcome those who would come to your party. This will start the evening off right, by throwing a scare into each and every one who approaches the party house. It also, as suggested above, makes everyone feel that to-night at least there will be no difference between one and the other, and that all are expected to join in the fun whole-heartedly.

If the room in which most of the games are to be played during the evening is fairly large, several of the skeletons may be used to hang around the walls of the room, and you will find it unnecessary to have many other decorations if a few skeletons are used. Especially if a large room or hall is to be used, such as the case might be, if a dance is to conclude the evening's fun, nothing would be more inexpensive, as an orginal decoration, than to use a number of these skeleton figures. The life-size skeleton is so jointed, that the arms and legs may be made to take most any particular position. This fact makes its use as a decoration most acceptable.

A skeleton hung in the corner with the eye sockets removed, and a light substituted for eyes will make a novel, as well as interesting decoration.

Just as surely as there is expected to be a ghost present at every Hallowe'en party, in order to scare every one present, at a definite appointed time, so too, a life-size skeleton can be used to suspend by a string from a cross string just inside the closet door, in the room, in which most of the playing is to be done. At some set time someone will be asked to get something from this closet, and the skeleton will then stand in full view. This is sure to shock many, and cause a great deal of merriment before everything can quiet down once more.

LIFE SIZE SKELETON
Original Stock No. 683
Initial Release: 1930
One design, 55" tall, 12" wide, printed black and white on cardboard die-cut, with all joints eyeletted, directions for use in decorating printed on back of body, each in a printed folding box envelope.
*Showing both sides of the box envelope. Note the handwritten notes made on the back of the box envelope.
Value: $110.00

DANGLING SKELETON
Original Stock No. 1784
Initial Release: 1938
Practical and interesting for the classroom and most popular decoration for party or store window perfectly reproduced from the real thing. Loose jointed – full size – 58" high.
*This is my favorite Beistle skeleton – he's facing you directly, not with a side glance like the others look.
Value: $110.00

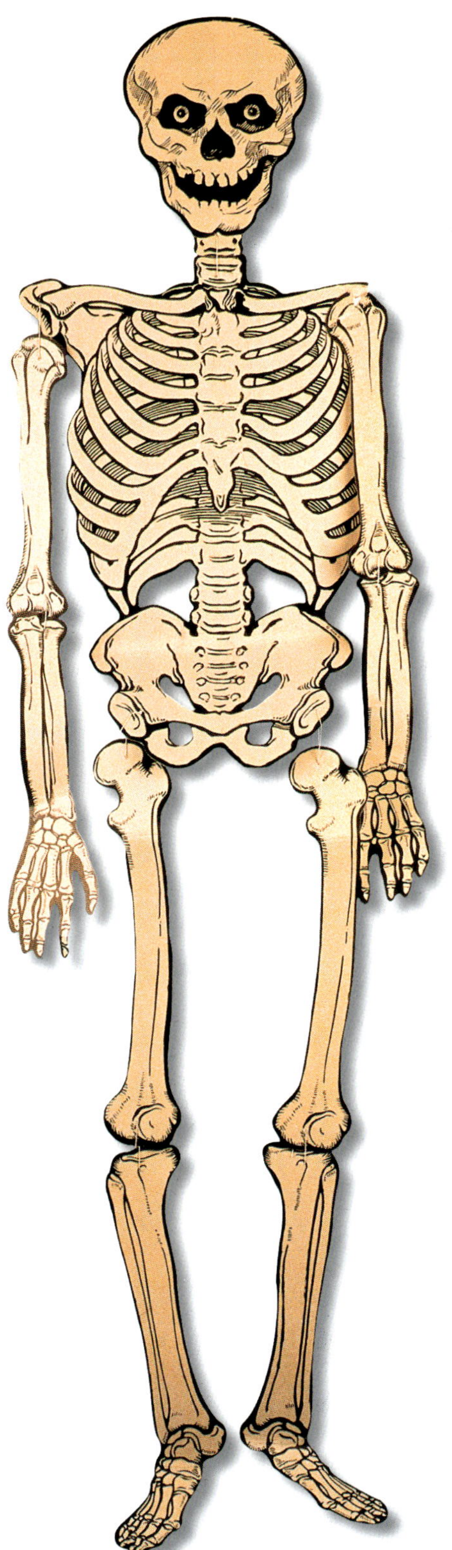

EMBOSSED SKULL
Original Stock No. 1111
Initial Release: 1941
Gruesome is the word for it! White cardboard embossed skull and crossbones with eyes, nose and mouth printed black. The size is 8.25" x 9.25".
Value: $55.00

LARGE NOVELTY CATS
Original Stock No. 1116
Initial Release: 1941
These novelty black cats stand upright on a cardboard base. The four different designs printed one side with orange eyes, nose and mouth. Average size 13" x 1".
*Since these pieces are rather large the archive folders couldn't contain them properly, hence the damage that can be seen in the photos. The value listed below is for pieces in excellent condition.
Value: $145.00 each

JOHNNY PUMPKIN HEAD
Original Stock No. 690
Initial Release: 1920
A grotesque brownie with an abnormally large pumpkin head slightly tilted with a comical expression. Measuring 5" high with a strong easel support.
*This particular design was introduced in 1920 as "The Johnny Pumpkin Head Family – Five Big Cheerful Brothers." Subsequently, Stock No. 691 was 8" high, No. 692 measured 11" high, No. 693 stood 16" high, and No. 694 came in at a whopping 20" high. Two examples are represented here.
Value: $55.00 – 210.00

4 JACK-O-LANTERN FACES
Original Stock No. 1806
Initial Release: 1940
Printed orange, black, yellow and green on heavy paper. Four separate smiling pumpkin face measuring 9" x 12." Each set contained in a printed Kraft bag.
Value: $165.00

DANCING FIGURES
Original Stock No. 1104
Initial Release: various
One design with head, hands and feet printed in colors on one side of the cardboard and joined together with orange and black honeycomb tissue body, arms and legs. Directions "How to Make it Dance" printed on back of each head.
*The classic-looking Witch was first issued in 1927 along with a black cat. In 1930, Beistle added to their line the Jack-O-Lantern Man. The happy Black Cat and the silly-looking Witch were issued in 1938. The Dancers were one of the earliest pieces Beistle produced and were so in demand that they continued to include them in their holiday line for many, many years.
Value: $115.00 each

LARGE EMBOSSED CAT MUSICIANS
Original Stock No. 1113
Initial Release: 1941
We've never offered a more attractive set of orange and black embossed cardboard decorations. Four large designs measuring 6" x 18.5".
*The Cat with guitar is shown with the set's paper wrapper.
Value: $95.00 each

MISS PUMPKIN HEAD
Original Stock No. 638
Initial Release: 1923
A new jointed Halloween Decoration joined with wire fasteners, measures 21" x 18" when opened, printed in bright Halloween colors.
*In its inaugural year of 1923, this little Halloween elf was introduced as "Miss Pumpkin Head." The piece was sold either with or without an envelope that was printed with an elaborate Halloween design in the inimitable Beistle style. The die-cut with envelope was listed as Stock Number 641.
*In 1925 this object was reintroduced as the Halloween Dancing Elf whereas in the 1927 catalogue it was dubbed "Pumpkin Doll." It reverted back to the Halloween Elf in 1930 where it reigned until 1932. As an aside, this piece would be one of the three most-favorite Halloween pieces in my collection.
Value: $950.00

HALLOWEEN WALL DECORATION
Original Stock No. 1536
Initial Release: 1934
Two designs measuring 11.5" x 29", printed in three Halloween colors and varnished on heavy stock. Die-cut, with 1" fringe at bottom and sides. Eyeletted holes at top with a string hanger.
*These pieces are absolutely magnificent! If I am ever fortunate to add either one to my collection you can bet that it will be professionally framed. The graphics are just jaw dropping! The third panel shown is an artist's offering that never went to press.
Value: $3,000.00 each
(Continued on following page)

HALLOWEEN CHARACTER HEADS
Original Stock No. 1555
Initial Release: 1933
Six designs measuring 12" x 12". Attractive Halloween character heads like Witch, Cat, Pirate, Jack-o-lantern, etc., printed in bright colors, embossed and die-cut with a hole at top of design for hanging.
Value: $110.00 each
(Continued on following page)

GIANT CAT AND JACK-O-LANTERN
Original Stock No. 1222
Initial Release: 1942
Two impressive display pieces that will give color and complete your Halloween decorating. Quite appropriate for any public or special party gathering. Printed in black and orange on heavy enamel paper. Made up two to a roll and each piece measures 24" x 36".
*These two pieces are HUGE and eye-popping. I'm lucky to have found the Jack-O-Lantern and I hope to find the Cat to complete the set.
Value: $225.00 each

"BLIX" THE HALLOWEEN OWL
Original Stock No. 1756
Initial Release: 1939
Use to stand on tables as a centerpiece, or on ledges, furniture, etc., as a decoration. If a string is looped through the hole provided at top, it can be hung as a room decoration.
Value: $185.00

"JITTER BUG" (a.k.a. HOT FOOT DANCER)
Original Stock No. 1767
Initial Release: 1939
Don't miss the new sensation of this season – the Jitter Bugs! Measuring 12" x 40" and printed on orange and black on cardboard. A laughing cat or pumpkin face with dangling arms and legs of folding honeycomb tissue in printed bag.
*I am showing the Laughing Cat along with three variations on their packaging.
Value: $175.00 each

SCARECROWS
Original Stock No. 1713
Initial Release: 1938
A new creation in wall decorations distinctly different! Four characters, cleverly designed and measuring 13.5" x 11.5". Printed cardboard parts with fringe arms and legs. Each in glassine bag with display card.
*There was a variation on this item – Stock Number 1718. It was the same as No. 1713 except the glassine bag contained an orange and black display card. The Witch in Photo #1 was introduced in 1939.
Value: $225.00 each
(Continued on following page)

EMBOSSED JACK-O-LANTERNS & CAT HEADS
Original Stock No. 1110
Initial Release: 1946
Quality, appearance, low cost! What a combination! Eight different designs printed in two colors, orange and black, and embossed on cardboard. These small cutout decorations can be used anywhere. Average size is 6" x 8.5".
*Five of the eight designs with one Grinning Jack-O-Lantern a repeat.
Value: $55.00 each

BIG SILHOUETTES
Original Stock No. 1570
Initial Release: 1936
Big, bold, horror pictures – 12" x 18" silhouettes, die-cut from black cardboard. They make a wonderful background or wall decoration for Halloween parties and displays.
*Stock No. 1571 is the same as above but the die-cuts were packaged in a glassine bag along with a display card (see photo #1). The last two photos show mock-ups where the Beistle artists applied the tangerine stock to the die-cut's openings (the Cat & JOL model), and created a shade-style with the transparent orange tissue (the Cat & Skull).
Value: $475.00 for complete set with display card

EMBOSSED HALLOWEEN PLAQUES
Original Stock No. 1109
Initial Release: 1941
A swanky new set of eight embossed cardboard Halloween plaques. Each plaque is printed in orange, black and yellow. Average size is 6.25" x 9.25".
*This is the set that I purchased in the late 1960s and which I still own today, although a bit the worse for wear.
Value: $25.00 each

HALLOWEEN TISSUE GHOST
Original Stock No. 1101
Initial Release: 1925
Halloween tissue ghost with folded tissue movable wings, heavy stock, die-cut. When open the piece measures 9-1/2" x 11-3/4" with a string holder. This is a new idea in a Halloween decoration.
*Two variations on the theme shown here.
Value: $185.00

HALLOWEEN JACK-O-LANTERN AND OWL

*The Owl die cut with moveable wings was first introduced in 1925 under Stock No. 622. The Jack-O-Lantern was first seen on the 1929 party game, "Jack-O-Lantern Fortune Wheel Game". These pieces were filed in the Beistle archives as a set but I can not find any evidence that this set was sold to the public.

Value: $145.00 each (if they can be found)

EMBOSSED CAT ORCHESTRA

Original Stock No. 1105

Initial Release: 1941

The eight different orange and black figures in this set of embossed decorations are made of heavy cardboard. Size 3.25" x 8.5".

Value: $225.00 for complete set

CHAPTER IV

GAMES

"The games she chose were from Beistle,
And were crowd pleasers – as she had planned."

JACK-O-LANTERN FORTUNE WHEEL
Original Stock No. 880
Initial Release: 1930
One design, 9", Jack-O-Lantern on Novelty rustic base that swings open ready to stand. Total height 12.5". Printed on cardboard with two number wheel spinners. Sixteen two-line fortunes printed at base for boys and girls. Directions printed on back.
Value: $125.00

"I'M A DUMB SKULL" STUNT GAME
Original Stock No. 881
Initial Release: 1930
One design, "I'm a Dumb Skull", 9.5" x 12.5", printed on cardboard with metal spinner at the base. Directions and stunts printed on back.
Stock No. 882
Same as No. 881 only each in a two color printed folding box envelope10" x 13".
*In the 1934-35 Beistle Line catalogue, the Stock Number changed to 1061 for the flat game and 1060 for the game with an easel. In photo #3 take note that the head on top of the skull changes from a parrot to a witch – this change was introduced in 1934.
Value: $125.00

WITCHES FORTUNE WHEEL
Stock No. 82
Initial Release: 1927
A new 15 cents Fortune Game – This Fortune Wheel is our latest creation and is different from all other fortune devices. It stands on a base and has paddle fortunes on the back. A Boy and a Girl can spin the wheel together and each have their fortune told at the same time. It has changes of positions so that the same couple spinning a second time will find different fortunes. Can be used to choose partners for Cards, Dinner or Games. It is a real Halloween amusement producer that will entertain the whole party. The ad goes on to say The Old Witch is pointing to the numbers on a spinning wheel. When the wheel is revolved two numbers appear, which correspond with printed numbers for a boys' or a girls' fortune that are on the paddles. Two paddles are eyeletted on the back and come out on either side. Full directions are printed on the back. The Witch is standing on a base of orange- colored honeycomb tissue paper, 8" in diameter. The whole game is 11" high.
*The game shown to the right, without a honeycomb tissue. base, was released in 1933 and given the Stock No. 1060. Beistle marketed four games in their Halloween line (the "Jack-O-Lantern Fortune Game," "I'm a Dumb Skull Stunt Game," "Witches Mystery Answer Board," and the "Witches Fortune Wheel") under one number beginning in 1933. They were simply called a "Game Assortment."
Value: $225.00

WITCH'S MYSTERY ANSWER GAME
Original Stock No. 1061
Initial Release: 1934
Four designs, four styles, 9.5"x 12.5", printed in Halloween colors and varnished on cardboard, die-cut, and with eyeletted spinner wheels. Directions on back of each. Other great fortune game with a series of printed questions, such as "Is he (she) a blonde?" and with a spin of the wheel a simple "yes" or "no" answer appears.
*One of four of the Halloween Game Assortment, this particular game was also dubbed "The Unconditional Oracle." Again, in 1938 the Stock Number was changed to 1060 and 1061 (1060 was the flat version of the game whereas 1061 sported an easel).
VALUE: $125.00

WITCH WHEEL GAME
Original Stock No. 1075
Initial Release: 1938
Watch the "Witch" move as you run the spinner and select a number. Fortunes for all, a clever, printed and die-cut novelty, 5.5"x 9.25".
*As the back of the game board suggests, each child "wheels it" at the table from one to the other. Amusing mechanical action for entertainment.
Value: $125.00

"WITCH" SPOT GAME
Original Stock No. 885
Initial Release: 1932
One design, Halloween number game called "Witch" with ten cards and numbers each different to be furnished the players, and with a supply of black spots used to cover the numbers as called. A master card of call numbers is furnished, together with a sheet of directions. All packed in a printed envelope 5.5"x 7".
Stock No. 886
Same as No. 885 only each in a covered two piece box 5.5"x 7.5" printed in Halloween colors.
Value: $125.00

MYSTERY ANSWER BOARDS
Original Stock No. 884
Initial Release: 1932
One design, size 5.75"x 8.5", printed on heavy cardboard in Halloween colors with attractive design, and with many suggested questions printed on the board. Cardboard spinner eyeletted in upper right hand corner, which is spun to get the answer to any question asked. Directions for playing printed on the back.
Value: $125.00

KITTY CARD GAME
Original Stock No. 61
Initial Release: 1928
The Game is made up of thirty cards in Halloween colors and intended for four players. Rules for playing the game are included in each box. Size of box is 4.5"x 5.25"x 1".
Value: $145.00

HALLOWEEN STUNT GAMES
Original Stock No. 875
Initial Release: 1931
One design, sixteen stunts, each on a card with Halloween design. Packed in a printed envelope 5.5"x 7" with directions and special instructions on the back.
Stock No. 876
Same as No. 875 only each in a two-piece covered box 5.5"x 7.5", printed in Halloween colors.
Value: $145.00

HOW TO USE THE STUNT CARDS

The inclosed 16 "stunt cards" are numbered serially 1 to 16. Distribute them among the guests, and then cut up the enclosed 16 numbers. Fold each number two ways, and place in a receptacle. In playing the game, pull one number out at a time, and have the guest, holding the card of the same number called, respond with the stunt called for on his or her card.

Another manner of distributing the cards, would be, to hold the tickets in your hand, and pass among the guests, asking each one to draw one. Then have them perform in numerical order beginning at No. 1.

SPECIAL INSTRUCTIONS

No. 1. Provide a 9 foot white string, and a pair of opera, or field glasses.
No. 2. Provide a round stick, or broom handle 30" long.
No. 3. Provide a glass of water.
No. 7. Provide an apple with a strong stem, and have 4 ft. of string tied to stem.
No. 8. Provide 9 ft. white string.
No. 9. Provide large apple, not too hard.
No. 10. Provide a candle and match.
No. 13 Provide a broom.
No. 14. Provide small stand, candle, match and sheet.
No. 15. Provide a doughnut, when asked.

PUMPKIN FORTUNE GAME
Original Stock No. 874
Initial Release: 1931
One design, twenty die-cut pumpkins printed in colors. On the back of each a number and four-line verse fortune, together with two sets of numbers used for mixing up the party. Packed in printed envelope 5.5"x 7" with directions printed on the back.
Stock No. 877
Same as No. 874 only each in a two-piece covered box, printed.
Value: $145.00

ZINGO FORTUNE AND STUNT GAME
Original Stock No. 1010
Initial Release: 1938
You can almost hear the roar of the crowd as the Spinner Wheel stops at your fortune or stunt. Measures 8.5"x 11.5" and printed on heavy cardboard.
*The game shown is an artist's mock-up…notice the green cardboard spinner.
Value: $165.00

HOO'S NEXT STUNT GAME
Original Stock No. 1104
Initial Release: 1941
Eighteen funny stunts are concealed under perforated stamps on cardboard printed orange and black. Measures 8"x 9".
Value: $110.00

STUNT QUIZ GAME
Original Stock No. 1103
Initial Release: 1941
Spinner wheel question and answer game. Cat points to question and owl to answer. Halloween colors of orange and black on cardboard measuring 8.5"x 9".
Value: $110.00

CRYSTAL FORTUNES GAME
Original Stock No. 1102
Initial Release: 1941
Spin the wheel, a number stops in the crystal ball and a corresponding number printed below tells boys and girls fortune. On heavy cardboard measuring 4.5"x 12".
Value: $110.00

WITCH STUNT GAME
Original Stock No. 1204
Initial Release: 1942
For real amusement and lots of fun- eighteen entertaining stunts concealed under perforated stamps. Printed in orange and black, measuring 7.75"x 9.5".
*As you can see, one of the JOL discs was popped off.
Value: $85.00

SPOOKY CAT GAME
Original Stock No. 1113
Initial Release: 1928
A new black cat party game – cat has loose legs and tail. Game is to place legs and tail over long eyelets in natural positions. Body, legs and tail die-cut from all black stock and enclosed in envelope 6.5" x 11" with design in colors and full directions on front.
*Stock No. 1112 is the same as above except very much larger – 8" x 13.375".
Value: $225.00 each

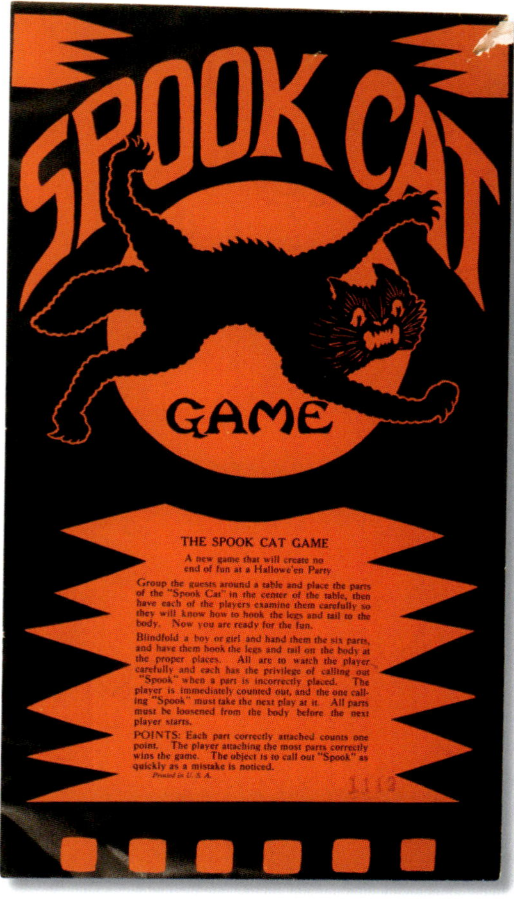

WITCHY GAME
Original Stock No. 1803
Initial Release: 1940
Measuring 5" x 9.5", this game is printed orange and black on cardboard. Black, orange and white ring on string with a funny printed jingle on the handle tells how to play the game.
Value: $135.00

FORTUNE STUNT PIE
Original Stock No. 1802
Initial Release: 1948
Something new. Tear out a piece of pie and between the crusts read a fortune and a stunt. Printed two colors on cardboard. Measuring 6" x 6", one design, assorted with three different sets of ten fortunes and stunts. Instructions printed on back of each.
*In the first photo, I am showing the front of the actual game along with two artist's mock-ups. Photo #2 shows the back of each game in the series.
Value: $85.00 each

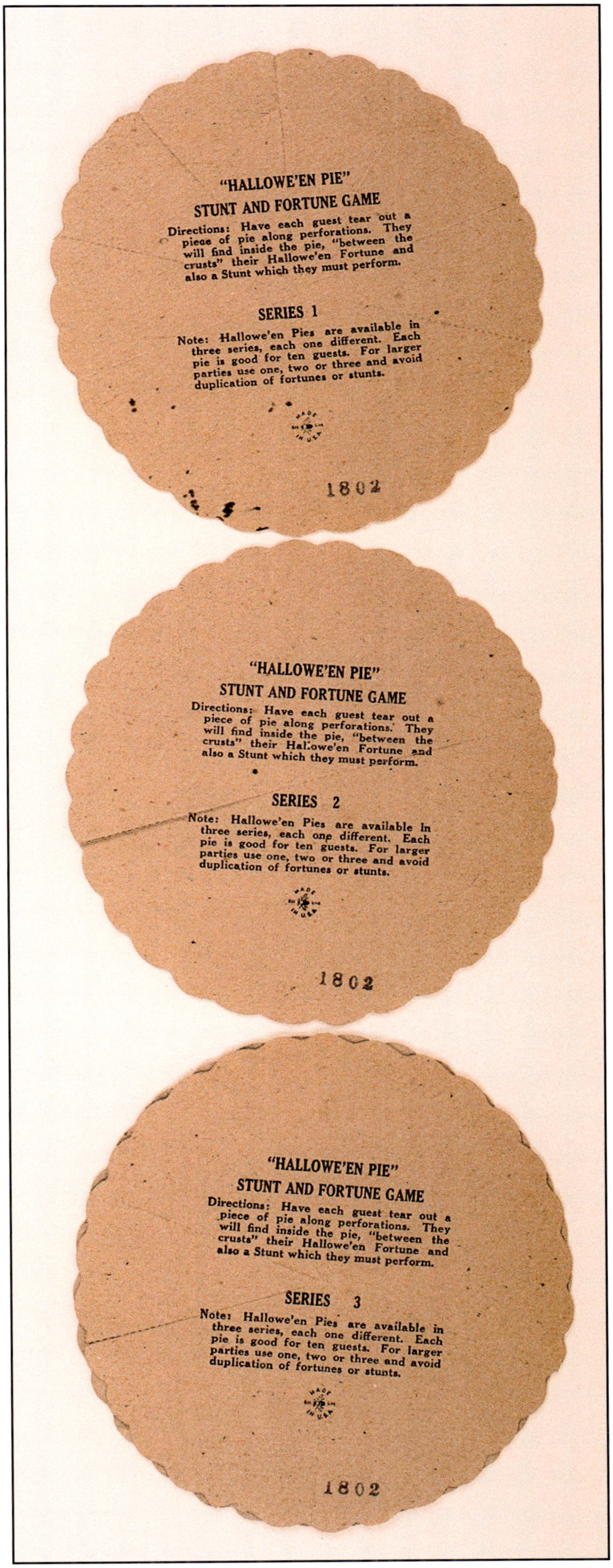

"HALLOWE'EN PIE"
STUNT AND FORTUNE GAME
Directions: Have each guest tear out a piece of pie along perforations. They will find inside the pie, "between the crusts" their Hallowe'en Fortune and also a Stunt which they must perform.
SERIES 1
Note: Hallowe'en Pies are available in three series, each one different. Each pie is good for ten guests. For larger parties use one, two or three and avoid duplication of fortunes or stunts.
MADE IN U.S.A.
1802

"HALLOWE'EN PIE"
STUNT AND FORTUNE GAME
Directions: Have each guest tear out a piece of pie along perforations. They will find inside the pie, "between the crusts" their Hallowe'en Fortune and also a Stunt which they must perform.
SERIES 2
Note: Hallowe'en Pies are available in three series, each one different. Each pie is good for ten guests. For larger parties use one, two or three and avoid duplication of fortunes or stunts.
MADE IN U.S.A.
1802

"HALLOWE'EN PIE"
STUNT AND FORTUNE GAME
Directions: Have each guest tear out a piece of pie along perforations. They will find inside the pie, "between the crusts" their Hallowe'en Fortune and also a Stunt which they must perform.
SERIES 3
Note: Hallowe'en Pies are available in three series, each one different. Each pie is good for ten guests. For larger parties use one, two or three and avoid duplication of fortunes or stunts.
MADE IN U.S.A.
1802

FORTUNE CRYSTAL GAME
Original Stock No. 1803
Initial Release: 1948
Spin the wheel, lift up the tab and read your fortune within the crystal. Printed in two colors on heavy cardboard. One design assorted with three different sets of twelve fortunes. Each game measures 5.5" x 6".
*Apparently Beistle made a fourth version of this game, #123, that was never released (which can be seen in Photo #2)..
Value: $95.00 each

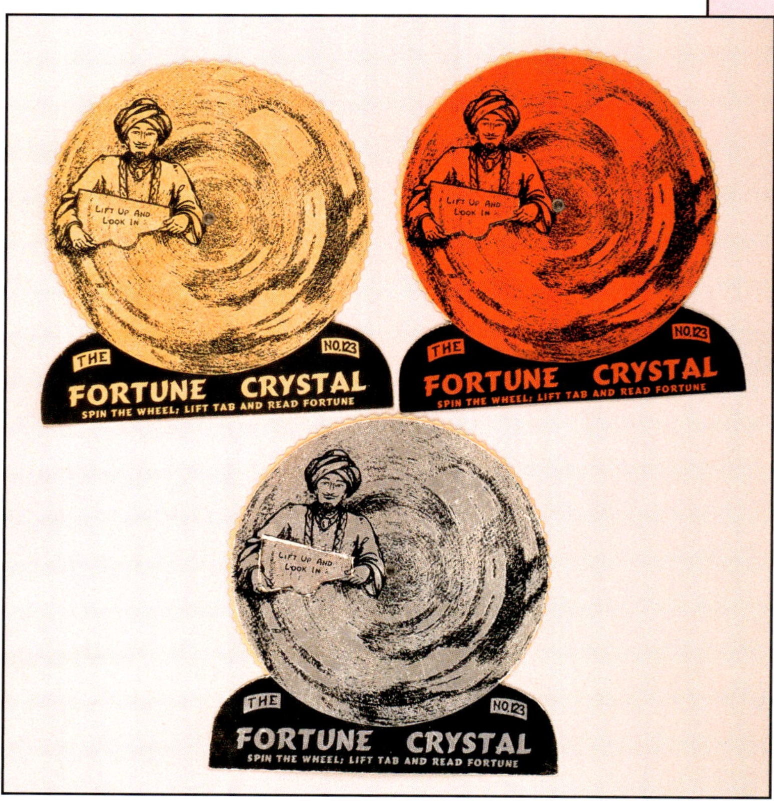

HALLOWEEN FORTUNES GAME
Original Stock No. 1902
Initial Release: 1949
Printed on heavy cardboard in orange and black, it measures 6.5" x 8". Spin the wheel, which reveals a number up to twelve, and refer to this number for your fortune.
Value: $135.00

HALLOWEEN RINGER STUNT GAME
Original Stock No. 1012
Initial Release: 1935
One design, six 6.25" x 7.75", consisting of 1 cat, 12 donuts and box container, printed in Halloween colors, varnished and die-cut from cardboard with directions and stunts.
*The boxed "Donut Game" was introduced in 1935 and lasted possibly until 1937. I unearthed a little treasure in the Beistle archives…this game packaged in a printed brown paper bag along with all its components. To the best of my knowledge, I don't believe this was ever marketed to the public.
Value: $175.00

CHAPTER V

PARTY HATS

"The Party Hats came in orange & black,
Decorated with Witch and Owl;
The partygoers simply looked their best,
And nothing was afoul."

HALLOWEEN HAT MASK
Original Stock No. 664
Initial Release: 1921
Four designs with tissue paper crown and mask 10.5" long.
Cutout eyes and nose to fit the face.
*The complete set is shown here.
Value: $145.00 each

HALLOWEEN HAT MASKS
Original Stock No. 85
Initial Release: 1928
Cardboard bands and meshed tissue crowns, full faces of Devil, Witch, Cat, Pumpkin Head, and Owl. Eyes, nose, and mouth are cut out with a long shredded tissue plume on each side.
*Two of the five styles are shown here (the Cat and Pumpkin Head).
Value: $125.00

PLUMED HATS
Stock No. 73
Original Release: 1931
Assorted four designs printed on 3.5" to 6" cardboard band, die-cut and with orange meshed tissue crown and two short orange tissue plumes.
*Two of the four designs showcased here.
Stock No. 74
Same as No. 73 except two long orange tissue plumes.
Value: $125.00 each

HALLOWEEN FIGURE HATS
Original Stock No. 87
Initial Release: 1931
Four assorted designs, 3.25" orange and black checkered cardboard band with spike crown of orange honeycomb tissue. Die-cut figures are attached to the front of hat – average size 10". These differ from Stock No. 88 in that these have two short orange tissue plumes.
*Two designs are shown here and again, I can't say enough about the spectacular graphics.
Value: $185.00 each

DOMINO HAT-MASKS
Original Stock No. 659
Initial Release: 1926
Four styles, Pumpkin, Bat, Owl, and Cat faces with black dominos. Each with orange- colored honeycomb tissue paper crown.
*The 1927 catalogue states, "The Domino Hat-Masks made their debut last season and judging from the repeat orders they must have become instantly popular. Why not? A Domino and a Hat in one."
Value: $145.00/each

PLUMED HATS
Original Stock No. 74
Initial Release: 1931
Assorted four designs printed on 3.5" to 6" cardboard band with orange mesh tissue crown with orange tissue plumes.
*Two of the four designs are shown here.
Value: $115.00 each

HALLOWEEN HAT
Original Stock No. 80
Initial Release: 1927
Halloween figures on the cardboard band. Orange colored clown-shaped crown and Cat and Witch on either side and a black-colored plume on top with orange-colored plumes on either side of band.
Value: $110.00

HALLOWEEN FIGURE HATS
Original Stock No. 88
Initial Release: 1931
*These hats are identical to Stock No. 87 except they do not have the short orange tissue plumes.
Value: $185.00 each

SPIKE CROWN HATS
Original Stock No. 70
Release Year: 1932
Assorted four designs printed on a 3.5" to 6" cardboard bank with orange meshed tissue spike-shaped crown.
*Two of the four designs shown here.
Value: $85.00

CLOWN SHAPED HALLOWEEN HAT
Original Stock No. 671
Release Year: 1923
Four new designs printed in Halloween colors, size 13.5" across and 15" high.
*Two designs shown here.
Value: $55.00

HALLOWEEN CLOWN HATS
Original Stock No. 671**
Release Year: 1925
Four styles all in bright Halloween colors, size 13.5" wide and 15" high.
*Apparently Beistle changed designs from year to year but "recycled" stock numbers, as in this case. Three styles shown here.
Value: $85.00

HALLOWEEN CLOWN SHAPED HATS
Original Stock No. 1180
Release Year: 1934
Four designs but one style measuring 11.5"x 15" printed in Halloween colors and varnished on heavy stock. Decorated cardboard band and enhanced with three tissue plumes.
*Four hats are in this set but each hat had two different designs. I think the graphics on these particular party hats are stupendous. Going through the archives, I haven't seen these particular figures repeated in subsequent years, as Beistle was wont to do on certain designs.
Value: $165.00 each
(Continued on following pages)

HALLOWEEN COOLIE STYLE HAT
Original Stock No. 1176
Initial Release Year: 1934
One design, one style measuring 12.5"x 12.5" printed in Halloween colors and varnished on cardboard, die-cut and with eyeletted guides and elastic cord to hold on head.
*The design on this party hat came right from the Beistle Halloween Party Outfit first distributed in the early 1920s.
Value: $145.00

TISSUE HATS
Original Stock No. 1041
Initial Release: 1933
Eight designs, soft shapes on orange colored tissue with a cardboard hatband printed with design of Jack-O-Lanterns in two colors and varnished. Halloween character design printed in black on one side of the hat and a six-inch plume on the opposite.
*One example of the design shown here.
Value: $125.00 each

HALLOWEEN ELF HATS
Original Stock No. 675
Initial Release: 1923
Four new designs of elves and pumpkins on front with hatband printed in Halloween colors with mesh tissue paper crown.
*These designs were also featured in the Beistle Halloween Party Kit, Stock No. 575, first issued the same year.
Value: $145.00 each
(Continued on following page)

HALLOWEEN PLUMED HATS
Original Stock No. 673
Initial Release: 1925
Two new styles, Pumpkin and Cat Head sides in full Halloween colors with orange and black tissue plume and orange and black tissue paper crown.
Value: $115.00 each

THREE-IN-ONE CLOWN SHAPED HAT
Original Stock No. 1083
Initial Release: 1933
Assorted two designs, size 12"x 18", clown-shaped, solid orange background with black Halloween silhouette character on both sides. With a perforated top 2.5" from the peak in which is attached a 12" orange or black tassel. When torn at this perforation, the top may be used as a shaker and the bottom as a megaphone.
*A truly clever idea!
Value: $115.00 each

CLOWN HAT
Original Stock No. 1797
Initial Release: 1940
Printed black on heavy orange stock with clown, witch, scarecrow, cat, and owl silhouette designs. Each measures 8"x 11.5".
*All five styles are featured here.
Value: $65.00 each

MOON FLAT HATS
Original Stock No. 1131
Initial Release: 1941
Colorfully printed cardboard hat assortment with four different black and orange designs. Spiked crowns of orange Art Tissue. Measures 5.5"x 11.5".
Value: $65.00 each

BAND SHAPED HAT
Original Stock No. 1173
Initial Release: 1933
One design printed with bright Halloween designs in four colors and varnished. Four-inch high cardboard band die-cut with an orange honeycomb tissue spike-shaped crown – with or without orange tissue plumes.
*Showing both front and back of the hat as well as the two styles, with or without the tissue plumes. I believe that this is one of the most intensely decorated Halloween hats that I came across in the making of this book.
Value: $165.00 each

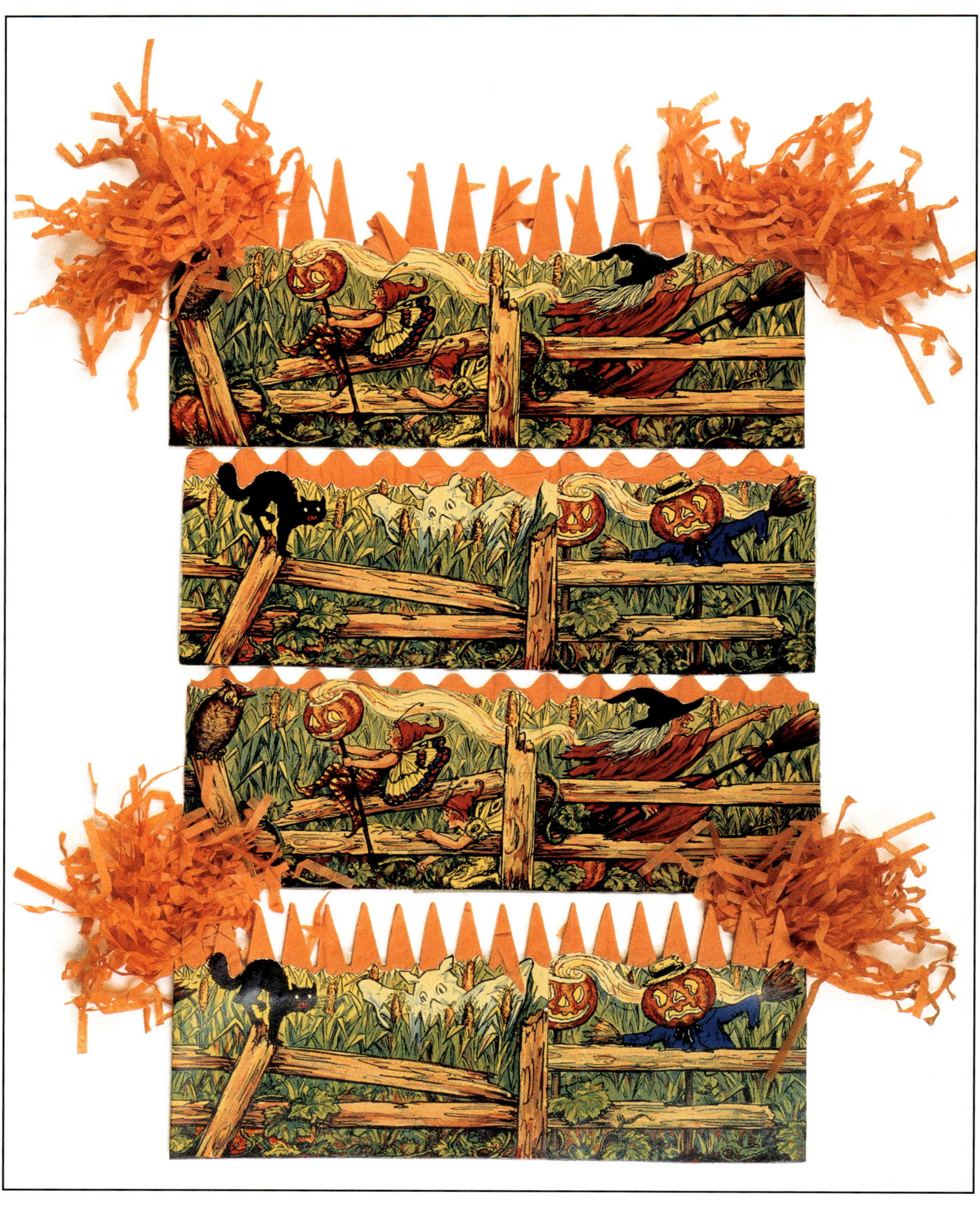

NEW MOON HATS
Original Stock No. 1192
Initial Release: 1933
Assorted four designs – Moons with Halloween Cats or Witches, and Halloween design band, all printed orange and black on heavy cardboard of orange and black, varnished and die-cut. Each with spike-shaped orange meshed tissue crown. Moon design measures 9"x 9".
*Some models had orange tissue plumes at each side.
Value: $125.00 each

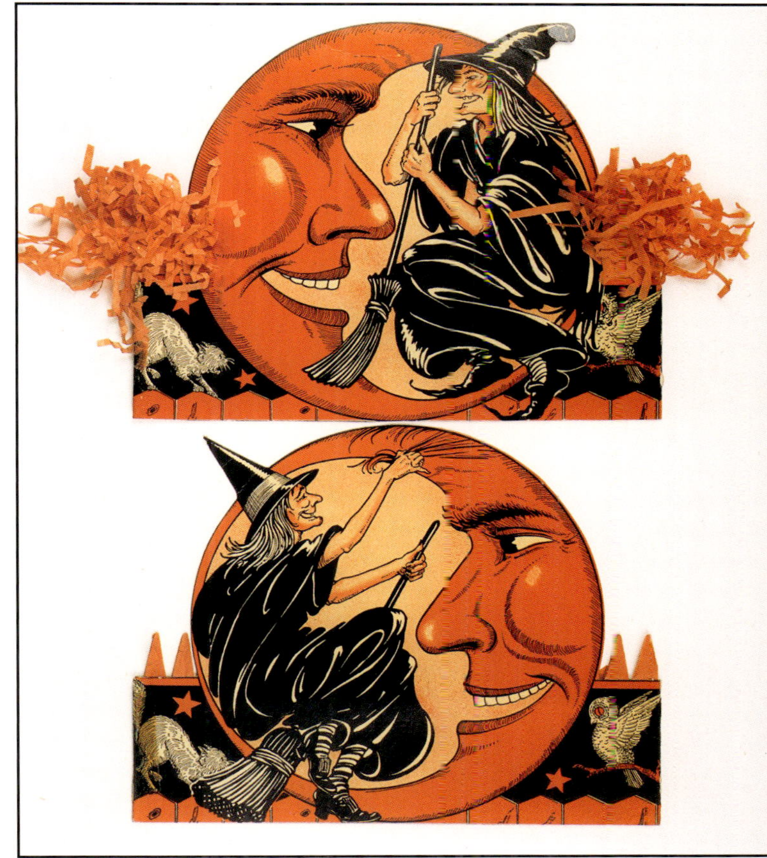

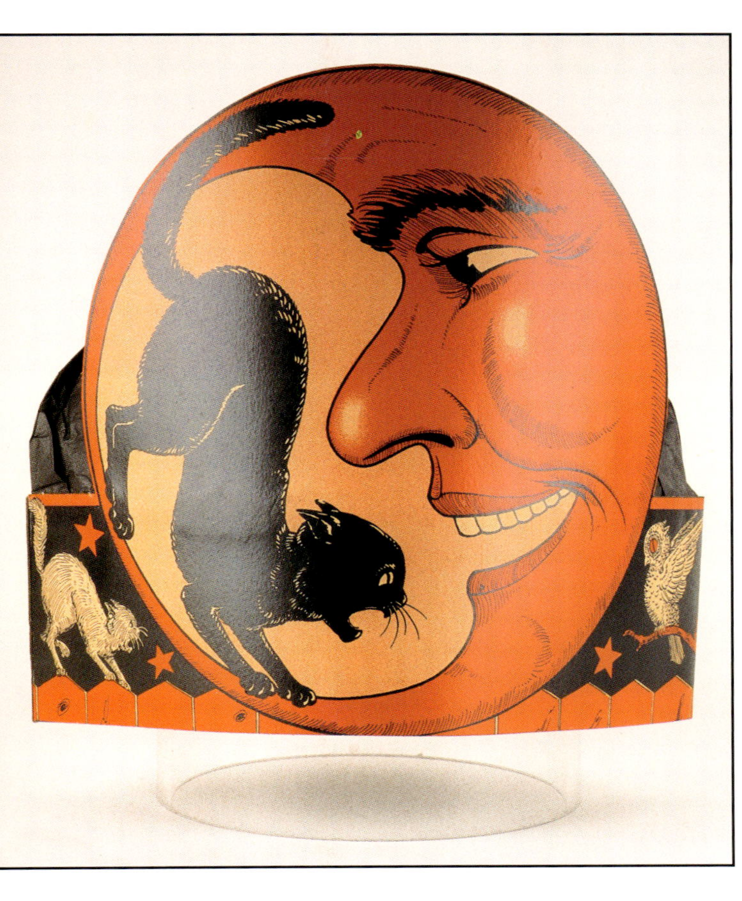

OWL AND CAT HATS
Original Stock No. 94
Initial Release: 1931
Assorted two designs measuring 11.5"x 11.5", printed orange and black on heavy white stock and die-cut, with heavy three inch hat band inserted.
*Examples in the photos shown with two or four plumes. Value is the same for either style.
Value: $115.00 each

MASK HAT
Original Stock No. 1724
Initial Release: 1938
Designed for greater value – natural color masks with die-cut eyes and nose on printed band with tissue crown. Four designs included in set.
*Three of the four designs are shown here. Beistle made full use of their designs – you'll never know where they'll turn up next!
Value: $95.00 each

CLOWN HAT
Original Stock No. 1731
Initial Release: 1938
The printed character designs strike a modern note in this durable clown hat with turned up brim and pom-pom decorations. Five designs included in set.
*I chose the three designs from this set that featured a "girlie" theme. When my sister Ri saw the photo for the first time she exclaimed, "Va-Va-Va-Broom!" I couldn't have put it better.
Value: $95.00 each

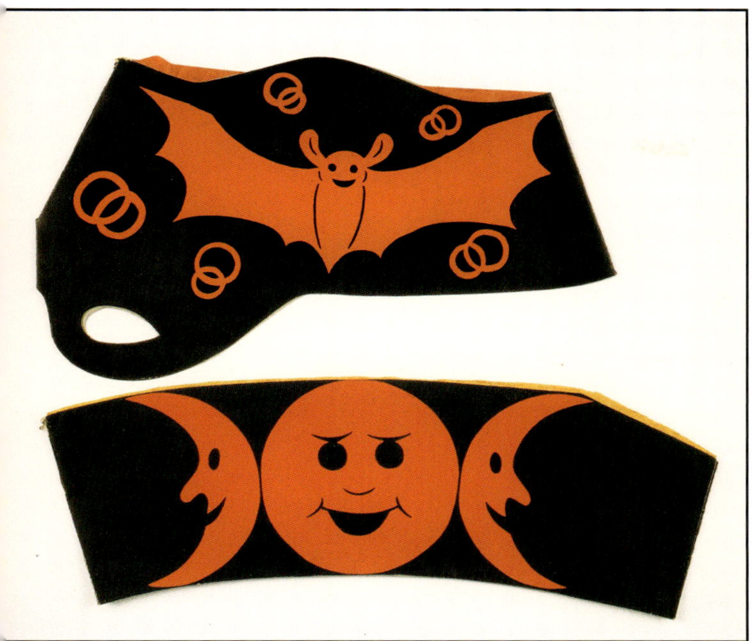

PRINTED HALLOWEEN FLAT HAT ASSORTMENT
Original Stock No. 1980
Initial Release: 1949
An outstanding assortment of six designs of cardboard hats printed orange and black. Full size with art-tissue crowns.
Value: $65.00 each

HALLOWEEN NOVELTY HAT
Original Stock No. 1737
Initial Release: 1938
Ladies, something new – an outstanding novelty – die-cut cardboard hats with printed characters on the brim.
*The photo doesn't show the Halloween silhouettes stamped on the brim of the hat. The hat's brim wasn't cooperating during the photo shoot!
Value: $75.00 each

SILHOUETTE PLAQUE HATS
Original Stock No. 1840
Initial Release: 1948
An outstanding silhouette flat hat. Printed orange and black on heavy cardboard, with full opening, die-cut crown. Decorated with Halloween designs and large silhouette plaques stitched to the front of the hat. Eight designs, size 6' x 12.5".
*Seven of the eight designs are shown here.
Value: $85.00 each
(Continued on following pages)

EEOOOwww

HALLOWEEN MASKS
Original Stock No. 1765-M
Initial Release: 1948
Ten attractive Halloween character designs, printed orange and black on cardboard stock with elastic thread to hold in place. Sizes average 10' x 11.5".
*Beistle also introduced these pieces without the eyes and nose cutouts as Stock No. 1705 in 1948 as "Halloween Faces". They suggested that these pieces could be used for wall decorations and/or party place mats.
Value: $75.00 each
(Continued on following pages)

MADE IN U.S.A.

MADE IN U.S.A.

CHAPTER VI
LANTERNS & SHADES

COMBINATION LANTERN
Original Stock No. 1118
Initial Release: 1941
Suggestions for use as a lantern, shade or stick lantern are printed on back. Black design on orange paper front. Size 6" x 12".
Value: $200.00

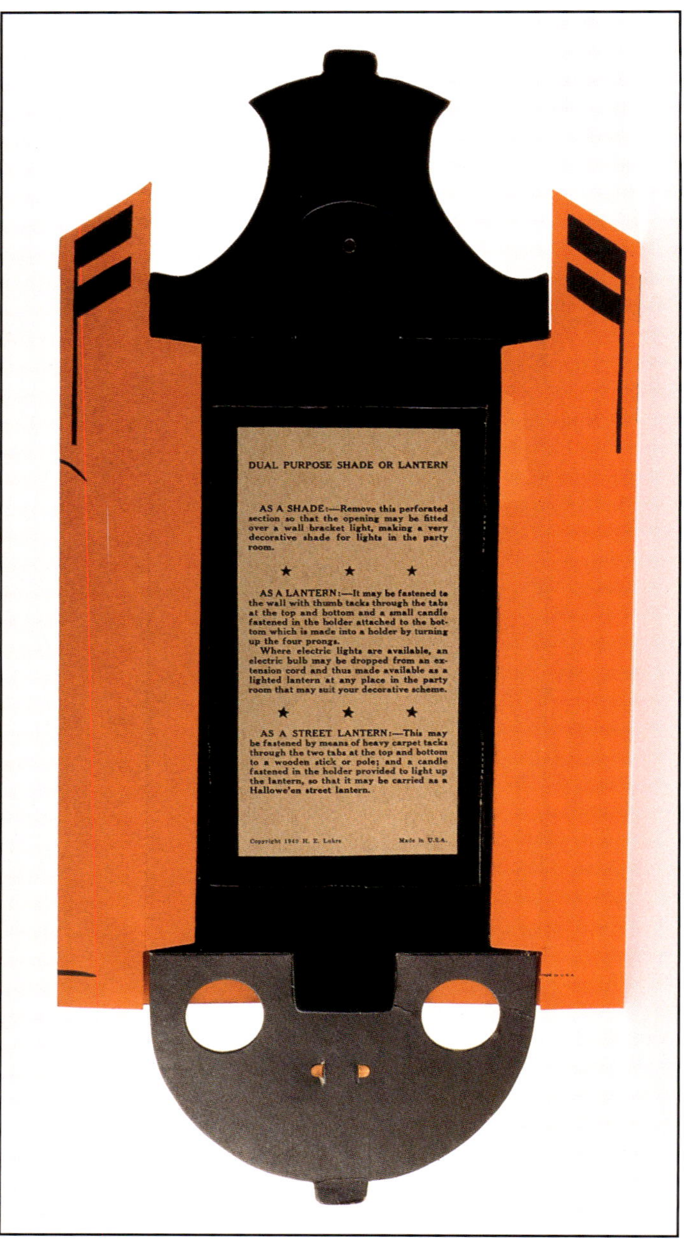

HALLOWEEN SILHOUETTE SQUARE LANTERN
Original Stock No. 101- 107 - 102
Initial Release: 1928
Die-cut silhouette panels lined with orange colored transparent paper, candleholder in bottom.
*This lantern (with the jack-o-lantern cutout on the very top) came in three sizes: 3.5" x 6.5", 4" x 8", and 4.75" x 9.5." Note the orange cardboard frame lantern in Photo #3 and #4.
Value: $65.00-145.00
(Continued on following page)

#11324
Crepe

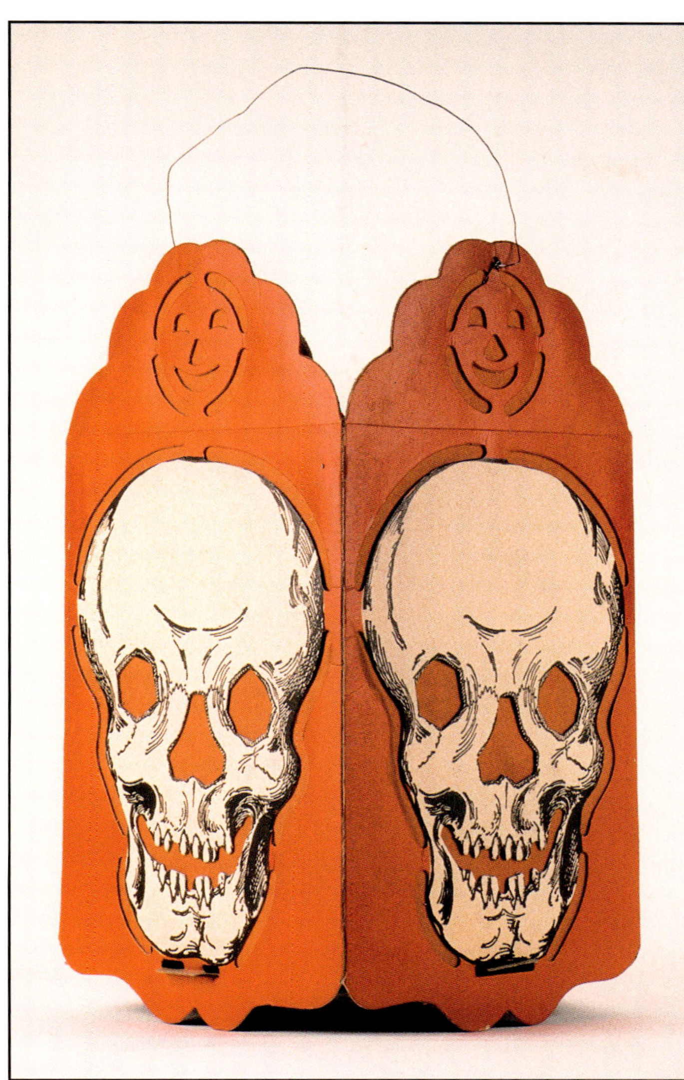

SKULL SQUARE LANTERN
Original Stock No. 109
Initial Release: 1931
One design, panel size 5.5" x 10.5", printed in orange and black on heavy white cardboard, and die-cut with a large white skull on each panel. Lined with orange colored transparent paper. Candle holder in bottom – wire bail at top. Suitable for an electric light.
Value: $110.00

SKULL LANTERN
Original Stock No. 1132
Initial Release: 1941
Black background and skull design printed on heavy white cardboard. Orange paper liner, candle holder, wire bail. Size 5" x 10".
Value: $110.00

LARGE SILHOUETTE LANTERN
Stock No. 1751
Initial Release: 1938
Large size, die-cut silhouettes with orange tissue liners, measuring 5.25" x 10". A big value!
*The cutouts at the lantern's top is that of an alternating Owl and Jack-O-Lantern.
Value: $165.00

SILHOUETTE SHADE
Original Stock No. 1117
Initial Release: 1941
Heavy orange paper shade with different black silhouette on each side. Cardboard top will fit any light fixture. Ten-inch orange tassels. Size 6.25" x 9.25".
*What spectacular graphics! The tassels had been removed when placed in the archival files.
Value: $165.00

STICK LANTERN
Original Stock No. 1815
Initial Release: 1940
Printed orange and black on cardboard with green Kraft paper liner. Wooden block attached to base bottom in which to insert stick and includes candleholder.
*This model came without the stick.
Stock No. 1815-S
*This model came complete with the stick.
Value: $375.00

JACK-O-LANTERN
Original Stock No. 1165
Initial Release: 1933
One design, size 11.5" x 12.5", natural Jack-O-Lantern design printed yellow, orange and black on heavy cardboard, varnished and die-cut with eyes, nose and mouth removed. The design is printed on both side of the lantern with orange or green transparent liner and with sides of cardboard with four metal fasteners to hold the lantern together. Collapsible for shipping but is readily set up and will hang or stand as desired. Fitted with candleholder in bottom and opening in top for electric light along with wire bail for use in hanging.
*Showing both versions with either the green or orange tissue paper liner.
Value: $165.00

SQUARE LANTERN
Original Stock No. 1160
Initial Release: 1933
One design, panel size 5.5" x 10.5" printed orange with black silhouettes varnished and die-cut with heavy cardboard. With a liner of orange or green colored transparent crepe paper. Each with candleholder in bottom and wire bail at top. Suitable for electric light.
*I am showing all four sides of this lantern in both the green and orange crepe paper inserts. Note the bat cutout at the top.
Value: $165.00

JACK-O-LANTERN
Original Stock No. 1154
Initial Release: 1933
One design, size 10" x 10.5", natural Jack-o-lantern design, each side different printed in yellow, orange and black on heavy cardboard. Varnished and die-cut with eyes, nose and mouth removed. Orange or green tissue transparent liners. Sides of cardboard with four metal fasteners to hold the lantern together. Collapsible for shipping but is readily set up and will hang or stand as desired. Each with candleholder in bottom and opening at top for electric light, and wire bale used in hanging.
*Two different expressions on this two-sided lantern. I am showing both sides with the orange and green tissue paper insert.
Value: $145.00

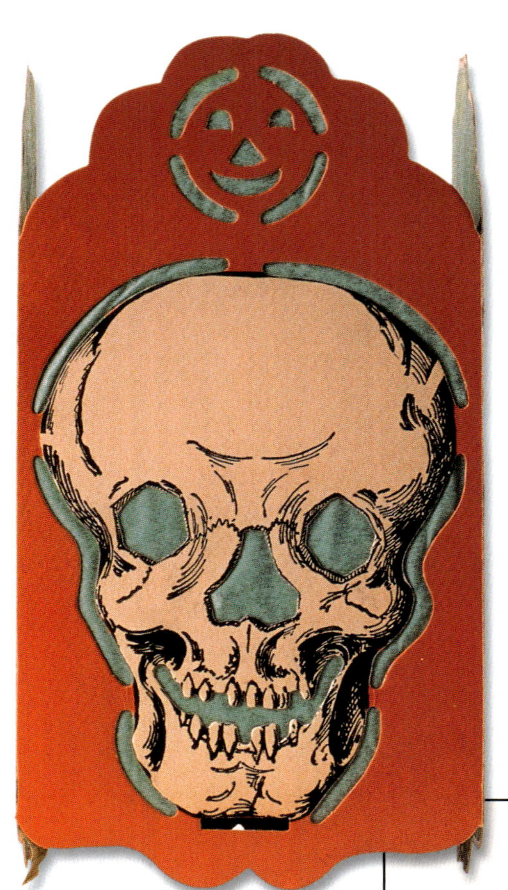

HALLOWEEN SKULL LANTERN
Original Stock No. 1155
Initial Release: 1934
One design, size 5.5" x 10.5" printed in Halloween colors and varnished on cardboard. Transparent tissue liners – each lantern with wire bail.
*A later variation on Stock No. 109.
Value: $110.00

TRIANGLE SHADE
Original Stock No. 1218
Initial Release: 1938
Effective simplicity makes this 7" x 8.5" shade a big seller.
*The three sides feature a cat, witch, and an owl. Notice the color variation in the one photo. I prefer the added yellow highlights, especially on the Owl panel.
Value: $110.00

PUMPKIN FACE SHADE
Original Stock No. 1219
Initial Release: 1938
Rich, gleaming transparent background with pumpkin face design on an oblong shade measuring 3.25" x 7.5".
*Showing two styles of this shade.
Value: $95.00

ROUND LANTERN
Original Stock No. 1215
Initial Release: 1938
We're especially proud of this lantern with queer faces and colorful transparency measuring 6.5" x 7".
*Two-sided with different expressions in a stained glass style. Showing two variations but the multi-colored truly stands out.
Value: $125.00

CAT LANTERN
Original Stock No. 1220
Initial Release: 1938
A nice pussy for Halloween – this black face cat is on a bright transparent background and makes an oval-shaped lantern measuring 5" x 7.25".
* Two-sided lantern with two different cat expressions.
Value: $125.00

COLLAPSIBLE LANTERN
Original Stock No. 1163
Initial Release: 1933
One design, four sides with printed black silhouettes on heavy tangerine cover stock with black cardboard top and bottom. Each side measures when open 8.25" x 6.5". Candleholder fitted in bottom and a large opening in the top for insertion of electric light. Includes a wire bail to hold in place.
Value: $145.00

TRANSPARENCY
Original Stock No. 1812
Initial Release: 1940
Printed orange, black and green on cardboard with yellow crepe paper liner and candleholder on cardboard base. Witch, cat and pumpkin face designs measuring 9" x 14".
Value: $195.00 each
(Continued on following page)

TRANSPARENCY
Original Stock No. 1813
Initial Release: 1940
Just a bit different! Same construction as Stock No. 1812 only smaller and with four designs printed in two colors, orange and black on cardboard with green crepe liner and candle holder on cardboard base. Owl, cat, witch, and pumpkin designs measuring 6" x 8.5".
*Note the difference between these examples which should be labeled lanterns (due to the candleholder base) and Stock No. 1813 (ca. 1940) which are true transparencies.
Value: $165.00 each

LANTERNS
Original Stock No. 1810
Initial Release: 1940
Printed orange and black on white cardboard with green Kraft liner candleholder and wire handle. Oval shape of cat or owl face designs measuring 10" x 13".
Value: $225.00 each

SMALL TRANSPARENCIES
Original Stock No. 1612
Initial Release: 1949
Same construction as Stock No. 1812 only smaller and with four designs of a witch, pumpkin, cat, and owl. Measuring 6" x 8.5" with yellow crepe liners.
Value: $195.00 each

ROUND PUMPKIN LANTERN
Original Stock No. 104
Initial Release: 1928
Heavy orange-colored cardboard with transparent eyes, nose and mouth for electric light or candles.
*This lantern came in two sizes: 8" and 12" in diameter. There was no mention in the catalogue that this was a two-sided lantern with differing expressions. Compared to the graphics of previous lanterns and even the die-cuts, this piece looks absolutely flat and lacks the creative flair shown in other Beistle Halloween items to date. Apparently the public thought so too since this lantern made its appearance in 1928 never to reappear. Due to this, the rarity factor greatly influences the value. Marked on the bottom "Made in Germany."
Value: $900.00+ (depending on size)

JACK-O-LANTERN
Original Stock No. 105
Initial Release: 1929
Diameter 12" printed on cardboard with transparent eyes, nose and mouth with honeycomb tissue folding sides, fitted for electric or candle light.
*In 1929, Beistle produced this lantern and "recycled" the stock number from the previous year's lantern that flopped, sales wise. Also this same year, Beistle only produced a 12" model of this JOL. In 1930, its stock number changed to #104 when it introduced the 8" model and the 12" reverted to the old stock number of 105. Confused yet?
In my opinion, the paper insert used only for this particular lantern far surpasses the examples utilized by the Germans in their lanterns and candy containers. If I had to pick three of my all-time favorite Halloween pieces from my collection, this fella ranks Number 1. To me, he just screams HALLOWEEN!
Value: $1,500.00+ (depending on size)

ROUND LANTERN
Original Stock No. 1210
Initial Release: 1936
One design measuring 10" x 11".
*For whatever reason, the items in the 1936 Beistle Halloween Sales catalogue were not given wordy descriptions. Showing both sides of the lantern in the photo. Also, note the artist's mock up with just the orange tissue paper insert in the top left photo, along with another mock up with notes in the bottom photo.
Value: $175.00

SCARECROW LANTERN
Original Stock No. 1719
Initial Release: 1938
You make no compromise with party decorations in this large lantern. Halloween characters are silhouetted in panels that reflect a soft orange background. Heavy cardboard printed and die-cut with tissue tassel, measures 9.25" x 9.25", 34" high.
*This was also dubbed "Ballroom Lantern" and to see it is to believe! It is HUGE and absolutely wonderful. Would love to have this in my collection. Photo #3 – the bare bones of a future Halloween lantern.
Value: $425.00

TRANSPARENCY
Original Stock No. 1820
Initial Release: 1940
A cone-shaped cat and pumpkin face wall decoration printed orange and black on cardboard with yellow crepe behind eyes, nose and mouth.
Value: $115.00 each

HALLOWEEN LANTERNS
Original Stock No. 1772
Initial Release: 1939
Cheerful Beistle lanterns help produce that gay Halloween party atmosphere! They are easy to sell when you display them – for candle or electric lights.
*These are really stunning; for whatever reason they only sold for the one year, 1939.
Value: $145.00 each

OWL INDIRECT SHADE
Original Stock No. 1716
Initial Release: 1938
Light up this beauty! It's a spectacular shade that serves as a highspot! Die-cut from heavy cardboard with a transparent liner, 10" x 10", cone shape.
*Stock No. 1717 is the same except with 11" orange tassel hanging from bottom. This is the model shown in the photo.
Value: $195.00 for either

SHADE
Original Stock No. 1789
Initial Release: 1939
Printed black and die-cut from cardboard with orange Kraft paper liner and orange tissue tassel. Three sides have transparent eyes, nose and mouth.
*Photo shows this shade along with its mock-up to the left. The model on the far right is sporting a fringe top that makes it look as if it has a crew cut!
Value: $235.00

HALLOWEEN SILHOUETTE SHADE
Original Stock No. 118
Initial Release: 1930
One design, size of panels 4.5" x 6", die-cut from solid black printed cardboard silhouette designs and with transparent tangerine tissue liner. Suitable for electric light – comes flat.
*Stock No. 128 is the same as No. 118 only constructed of heavier cardboard. The photo shows Stock No. 118.
Value: $115.00 each

PUMPKIN LANTERN
Original Stock No. 1910
Initial Release: 1949
Small oblong shape, a smiling or frowning pumpkin on either side printed orange and black with green tissue liner. Lantern measures 5" x 8.5" and comes with wire bail and metal candleholder.
*In both photos, the Pumpkin Lantern is flanked by artist's models on either side.
Value: $115.00

HALLOWEEN LANTERN SHADE WITH TASSELS
Original Stock No. 1785
Initial Release: 1939
Colorful Beistle Halloween shades are ideal for quick "dress" in rooms where electric fixtures are used. Easy to apply – they quickly add color and gaiety to any setting.
*Photo shows four-sided black lantern with orange tissue liner along with its mock-up in white. This model was offered to the buying public in 1939 only.
Value: $175.00

TRANSPARENCY
Original Stock No. 1613
Initial Release: 1949
Printed orange and black on cardboard with green crepe liner.
Owl, cat, witch and pumpkin design.
Value: $165.00 each
(Continued on following page)

JACK-O-LANTERN
Original Stock No. 1808
Initial Release: 1940
*This is a variation on the above model. It appears that the artists at Beistle were always rethinking their designs. Along with the original artist's sketches, there is an attempt to make #1808 into a box lantern. They tried this idea on a few of their best sellers, as you will see in the next listed item. As of 1949, where my book "pauses," this item was never marketed to the public.
Value: Priceless

JACK-O-LANTERN
Original Stock No. 105
Initial Release: 1929
*Another attempt to recycle one of Beistle's popular Halloween items. Two variations on the tissue paper insert. Again, to the best of my knowledge, this box lantern was never marketed....and I am very, very disappointed!
Value: Priceless

MISCELLANEOUS

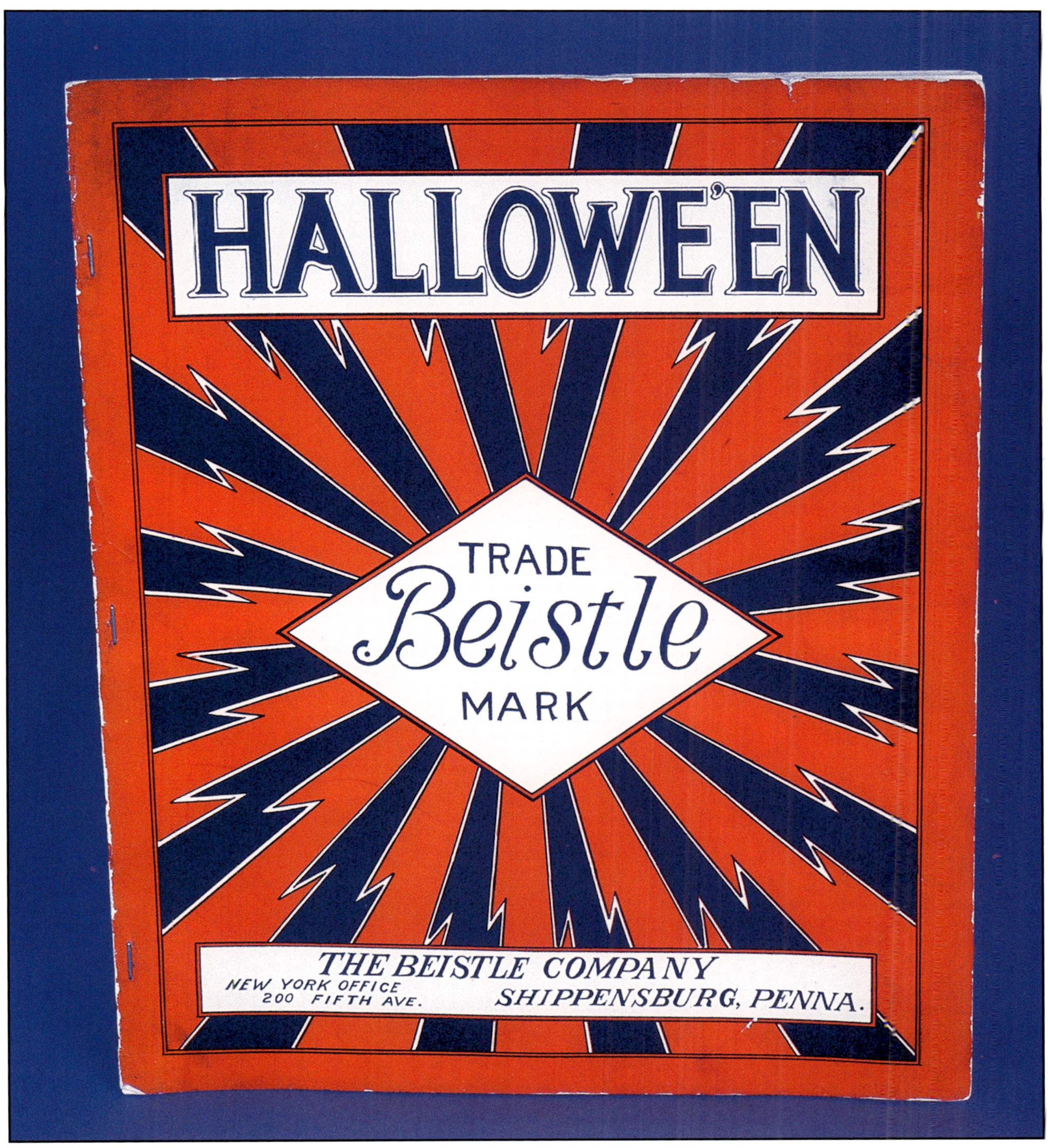

The cover of the 1929 Beistle Company Halloween Sales Catalogue. It's very graphic and a real eye-catcher.

8 The Beistle Company, Shippensburg, Pa.

The Johnny Pumpkin Head Family
Five Big Cheerful Brothers

No. 690 No. 691 No. 692 No. 693

690 Johnny Pumpkin Head— Per Gross 90

691 Johnny Pumpkin Head— Per Gross $2.25

692 Johnny Pumpkin Head— Per Gross $4.50

693 Johnny Pumpkin Head— Per Gross $9.00

See Front Cover

694 Johnny Pumpkin Head— Per Gross $13.50

A page from the 1920 Beistle Company Halloween Sales Catalogue where the family of "Johnny Pumpkin Head" was introduced..

The Beistle Company
Manufacturers
Honey Comb Tissue Valentines, Everything for the Hallowe'en Party, Paper Hats, Christmas Paper Novelties, and Filled Easter Baskets.
SHIPPENSBURG, PENNA.
New York Sales Office, 200 Fifth Avenue. Season 1927

1927

Oh, Boy!
What a Hallowe'en Line Beistle is making.

It beats the

The cover of the Beistle Company 1927 Halloween Sales Catalogue. Again, great graphics and I love the notation at the bottom featuring one of their new (for 1927) items, "Old Nick".

The Beistle Line

Hallowe'en Decorations

Allow us to introduce Mr. Johnny Pumpkin Head and his four sturdy brothers---See outside cover.

THE BEISTLE COMPANY
MANUFACTURERS
SHIPPENSBURG, - - - PENNA.

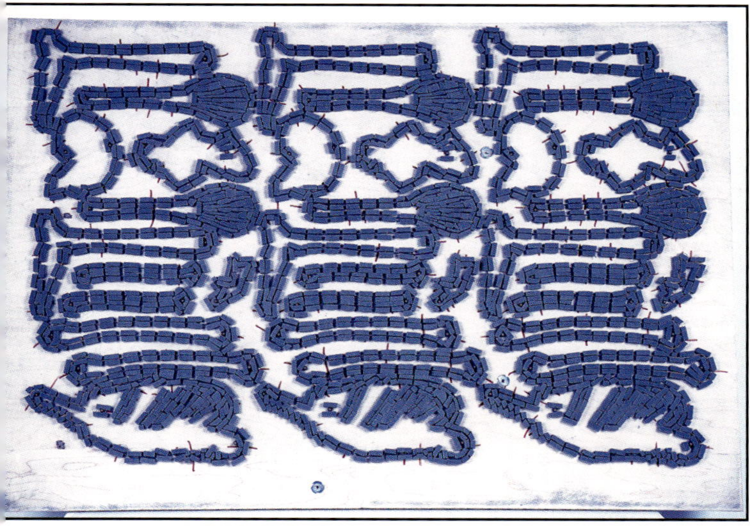

Beistle Die Boards

I thought you might be interested in seeing how a die-cut is created. The first two photos show "Profile Pete" which is one of Beistle's latest Halloween die-cuts. I thought it'd be a hoot to have Pete pose on the reverse side of his die board. He was just a little too eager to oblige as the second photo attests. If you look closely at Photo #3, you will certainly recognize the outlines that are the set of eight Embossed Halloween Plaques, Stock No. 1109, introduced to the public in 1941.

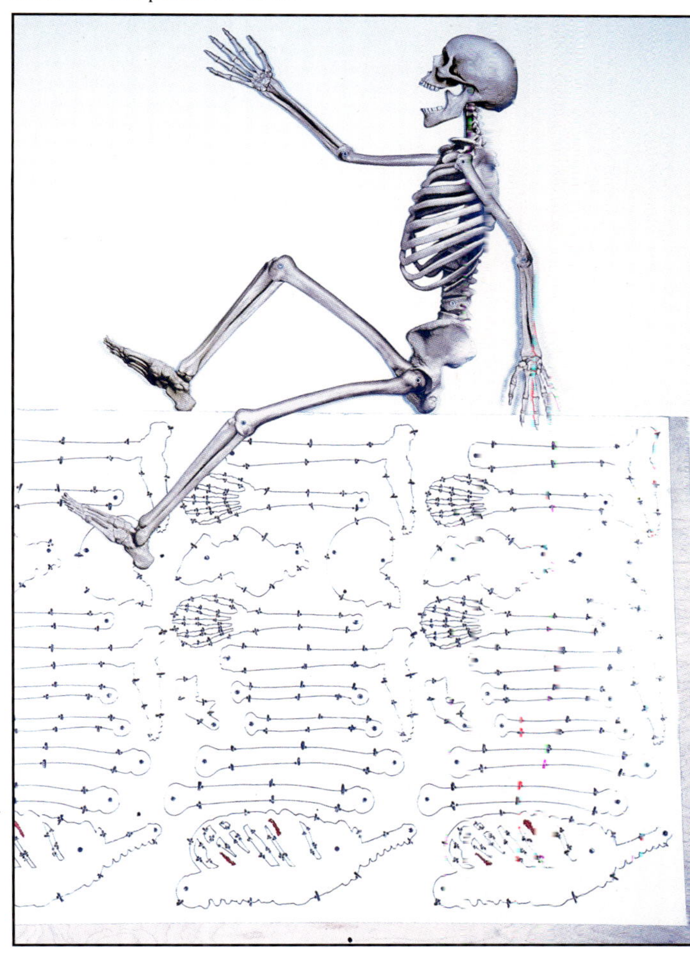

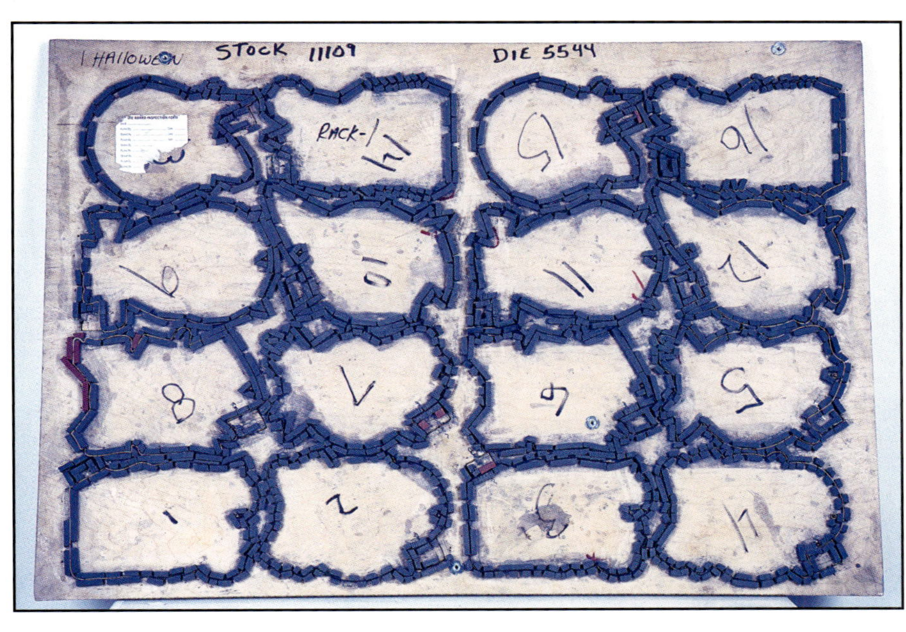

The Pumpkin
by John Greenleaf Whittier
(1867)

Oh – fruit loved of boyhood! – the old days recalling,
When wood grapes were purpling and brown nuts
were falling!
When wild ugly faces were carved in its skin,
Glaring out through the dark with a candle within!